THE WATERWAYS OF
Sydney Harbour

THE WATERWAYS OF
Sydney Harbour

PHILLIP MATHEWS

Phillip Mathews
BOOK PUBLISHERS

First published 1997 by Phillip Mathews Book Publishers Pty Ltd
80A Willoughby Road, Crows Nest, NSW 2065

Distributed by Boat Books Pty Ltd, telephone (02) 9439 1133 fax (02) 9438 8517

Copyright © Phillip Mathews Book Publishers Pty Ltd
Text, charts, illustrations: Phillip Mathews.
Photographs: Reg Morrison, Phillip Mathews
Printed in Hong Kong
ISBN 0 646 32969 3

ABOUT THIS BOOK

*T*HIS BOOK OFFERS useful information for boating people and those generally interested in the harbour. It is not intended as an alternative to the precision of RAN Charts. Anyone navigating the harbour should refer to the RAN chart *Aus 200*. This book's purpose is to help the reader to decide where to go; where to anchor; what boating facilities are available; what shores offer recreational use; how to reach the chosen spot by road if meeting friends; and background information on the harbour's many bays, coves and promontories. There is always somewhere on the harbour that offers shelter from the prevailing winds and a variety of fascinating outlooks, many more than most realise. Recreational boating enthusiasts tend to particular or familiar parts of the harbour, yet there are 250 kilometres or shoreline to explore.

For those confused by the fundamental distinction between Port Jackson and Sydney Harbour, the Admiralty Sailing Directions should, quite properly, have the last word:

> *Port Jackson is the name given to all the whole of the waters within an imaginary line drawn from Outer North Head to Inner South Head. Sydney Harbour is the name given to all Port Jackson except North and Middle Harbour. The limits of the Port of Sydney are defined as all the area westward of an imaginary line joining Inner South Head and Middle Head.*

There you have it. Precisely. If Sydneysiders know this, they cheerfully ignore it. They call North Harbour, "Manly", Middle Harbour correctly, and the rest of Sydney Harbour just "the harbour". If a distinction is made, it is likely to be "this side of the bridge" or the "other side". And that's OK. But if you want to really explore the harbour, then it helps to be more exact. For easy reference, this book is divided into The Entrance, North Harbour, Middle Harbour, the Lower Harbour (east of Sydney Harbour Bridge) and the Upper Harbour (west of the bridge), including the readily navigable waters of the Lane Cove and Parramatta Rivers.

Of the many texts referred to in compiling this book, two were invaluable. Firstly, P.R. Stephenson's definitive work, *The History and Description of Sydney Harbour* (Rigby, 1966). A revised edition, supplemented by Brian Kennedy after Stephenson's death in 1965, was published in 1980 by AH and AW Reed. Secondly, Alan Lucas's *Sydney to Central Coast Waterways Guide,* currently out of print. Lucas is *the* authority on cruising guides. He leaves large footprints, which I followed with deference.

In compiling the charts for this book, many of the symbols and abbreviation conventions of Admiralty Charts (there are 70 pages of them!) were ignored as too complicated for its user-friendly purpose.

Soundings are given to the nearest half-metre: thus 2+ indicates between 2 and 2.5 metres; 3- indicates between 2.5 and 3 metres, and so on. Does anyone really cruise the harbour taking sufficient bearings to establish the exact position of, say, an Admiralty sounding of 2.7 metres? And do they then calculate how many centimetres the prevailing tide has altered it. I think not. Soundings are a guide but the writer can assure readers that those marked in the harbour shallows on the charts herein were laboriously checked — with a lead line! — over 6 months.

In fact, every reasonable effort was made to make the information here accurate and useful. Having said that, no guarantee can be given nor responsibility taken for unintended inaccuracy. The harbour continually changes.

The publishers welcome constructive suggestions from readers for future editions.

PHILLIP MATHEWS

CONTENTS

CONTENTS

SYDNEY HARBOUR

"...the finest harbour in the world
in which a thousand ships of the line
may ride in perfect safety".

SYDNEY HARBOUR is one of the biggest, most secure, and arguably the most beautiful harbour in the world. A splendid natural inlet on Australia's east coast, it was the site of the First Settlement and it remains the focal point for the nation's biggest city. Robert Hughes, author of *Fatal Shore*, described the harbour as Sydney's womb. It might also be described as the nation's.

Though named Port Jackson, the official nomenclature is ignored by most. To Australians in general it is Sydney Harbour. To Sydneysiders it is just The Harbour.

Technically, it lies at Lat. 33°52' South, Long. 151°12' East, in the Southern Hemisphere's temperate zone. And it is blessed with a climate to match, similar to that of the Mediterranean or Southern California.

The harbour's broad entrance spans about 1.5 kilometres between the towering cliffs of North and South Heads. Ocean swells heave through it to dissipate in Middle Harbour. The rest of the harbour is landlocked, and well-sheltered from the elements by the coastal sandstone ridge. This tidal refuge covers nearly 50 square kilometres. Its foreshores, an irregular chain of bays and coves, separated by promontories, stretch nearly 250 kilometres.

The harbour's three estuarine arms converge in a deep sound, just inside the entrance. North Harbour sits in the lee of North Head; Middle Harbour faces the entrance and winds away in a generally northwesterly direction, to Middle Harbour Creek.; and the Main Harbour, in the lee of South Head, extends for some 24-kilometres east-to-west, from Watsons Bay to the narrows of Parramatta River.

The harbour is a flooded valley, shaped by the confluence of the Lane Cove and Parramatta rivers and, to a lesser extent, Middle Harbour Creek. Cut deep by the scouring of the sandstone terrain by endless tides and freshwater floods, perhaps influenced by tectonic movement and volcanic subsidence, the result is a fjord-like basin surrounded by steep wooded ridges, particularly along its northern shores.

The generous width between the northern and southern shores is about 1.5 kilometres, ample sea-room for its two navigation channels, the depths of which are around 12 metres, sufficient to accommodate the larger vessels.

The vast majority of the harbour is readily navigable for recreational boating, almost to the water's edge, even in most of the many coves and bays. In fact, more than half of the harbour is around ten metres deep. (The depth between the heads at the entrance is about 25 metres.) Tides are similarly benign, having an average rise and fall of about 1.5 metres and for the most part running at under a knot, though it marginally exceeds this near the entrance.

Around the shores of the Harbour lies metropolitan Sydney, which sprawls from the ocean beaches to the Blue Mountains. It is the oldest white settlement in Australia with a strong maritime tradition. In the first 20 years of its settlement, initially as a penal colony, its first four governors were naval officers — Phillip, Hunter, King and Bligh. To that extent it was a naval operation before the mercantile element of the port grew with the colony.

Australia is a largely immigrant nation and its major population centres still cling to its sea shores. Its dependence on the shipping routes was forged in the first hundred years of white settlement, when its isolation from Europe was most keenly felt. The colony was dependent on shipping for survival, not to mention development. Settlers, soldiers, convicts, trade and mails: all sailed the 21000-kilometre sea route from Europe, usually from Britain. If the early convicts and their keepers were reluctant voyagers, they had good reason, not the least being the perils of the deep. They were at sea for months, including the wild southern latitudes, crammed in small, insanitary ships, often of doubtful seaworthiness.

Whatever their fears for the future, relief must have been absolute when they finally sailed beneath the bold cliffs of the entrance into the snug safety of the harbour. Relief too for the colonists. The sight of a sail was cause for great joy: they had not been abandoned.

Some 8 kilometres west of the entrance, the Main Harbour is spanned by the Sydney Harbour Bridge, which links the commercial centres of Sydney and North Sydney. It also divides the Main Harbour into the Upper Harbour (westward) and the Lower Harbour (eastward).

Though there are a number of islands in the Main Harbour, notably Shark, Clark, Fort Denison, Cockatoo, Goat and Spectacle, the harbour's freshwater tributaries deposit remarkably little silt. It is largely free of sandbanks or reefs to obstruct navigation. The glaring exception is Sow and Pigs Reef near the entrance, which is well marked, well lit and easily avoided.

The landscape of the harbour's foreshores is an irregular mix of development, largely residential, and protected strips of bushland, much of which is part of the Sydney Harbour National Park.

As the city grows, the need to protect the foreshores becomes increasingly acute, though by world standards the port of Sydney has remarkably picturesque shores, minimal industrial development and relatively clean waters.

Even in the main harbour, much of which is developed to the water's very edge — particularly along the southern shores — the north shore has retained kilometres of steep wooded slopes, rising from the water to the brow of the escarpment in an almost unbroken belt of bushland: the longest stretch runs from Little Sirius Cove to Bradleys Head, and on to Middle Head and Balmoral in Middle Harbour. If the passing harbour sailor finds this soothing, a hike along its quiet bush tracks is near transcendental for the citizens of a frenetic metropolis. The southern shore is less fortunate, notable exceptions being the picnic area of Nielsen Park, and the delightful, carefully cultivated sweep of Farm Cove, from Mrs Macquarie's Chair (or, more correctly, Point) to the Sydney Opera House. And off the southern shores, Clark Island and Shark Island offer shady sanctuaries.

Some contend that harbourside development

creates the character of the harbour. Certainly the splendid homes of the privileged at Darling Point and Double Bay tend to fascinate visitors and divert the concentration of yachtsmen as they circle before the start of weekend races. Some buildings enhance, or at least blend with, the shorescape. Others diminish it, sometimes shamefully, including some particularly vulgar developments of 1950s and '60s. Little wonder that harbour development of any kind now raises bedlam the moment it's mentioned.

Many who appreciate the harbour as a working port fear that it might ultimately lose its maritime character with a sharply reduced navy and military presence, and abandoned heavy shipyards, docks and wharves, not to mention the myriad small boatsheds and marinas priced out of the existence by the disproportionate value of the real estate they clung to.

At the time of writing, the Defence Department was vacating harbour foreshore sites at Middle Head and Georges Heights, Woolwich and Cockatoo Island. Similar uncertainty surrounds the 4.5-hectare site at Balls Head, dominated since 1916 by its coal loader jetty. Leased from the State by BP for oil terminals, the lease expires in 2005, though coal loader has been vacant since 1992.

The historic wharves at Pyrmont and Walsh Bay are to be retained but it is doubtful that they will serve any maritime purpose.

The harbour's biggest island, Cockatoo Island, which lies between Clarkes Point, (Woolwich) and White Horse Point (Balmain) is as rich in local history as it is uncertain in its future. Till recently a busy dry dock and workshop, the island served as a convict barracks early in the 19th century before the Fitzroy and Sutherland Dry Docks were built, along with the defunct power station. The dry docks, though still in working order, were abandoned as uneconomical a few years ago. Now, even Sydney Harbour ferries have to be sent to Newcastle for servicing.

The debate about Cockatoo Island's future

SHARKS IN THE HARBOUR

Despite grim warnings from harbour fishermen there have been only four serious shark attacks in Sydney harbour in nearly 40 years: a 13-year-old boy snorkelling at Roseville was taken in 1960; three years later, Sydney actress Martha Hathaway was killed by a shark in knee-deep water near Sugar Loaf Bay; two divers survived a mauling in Berry Bay in 1972; and in 1996, 24-year-old Darren Good survived a shark bite on the thigh while swimming the Parramatta River. It may be less than reassuring, but only 16 people are known to have been killed by sharks in the harbour since First Settlement.

In recent years, two attacks have been made on rowing sculls (though not the rowers), perhaps because their swift, slim lines seem more like a marine creature from below. A large shark bit the stern of a Sydney Boys' High School boat in 1996 in Glades Bay, in the upper reaches of the harbour. The following year, Andree Moscari was thrown from her scull when a shark attacked it in Iron Cove.

None of these sharks was identified, though there was no shortage of opinion.

There is plenty of anecdotal evidence, particularly from fishermen, of sharks being present in the harbour, though most harbour yachtsmen will admit they've never seen one. The only certainty is that sharks do enter the harbour in unknown numbers and frequency. Some claim bronze whalers enter Middle Harbour to breed.

If this seems frightening, it needs to be put in perspective. Not all sharks are threatening. And vastly greater numbers of sharks exist off our ocean beaches, yet it doesn't prevent millions enjoying the surf every year. The odds of being attacked anywhere by a shark are astronomical when compared with the risk of road death or fatal home accidents. The chances of being attacked by a shark in the harbour is even more remote. You are more likely to be struck by lightning.

If your fear of sharks is acute, no reassurance will help; but if you do choose to swim in the harbour, drowning is a much more realistic concern. On the other hand, of course, there are no guarantees.

continues but if it is sold for private development it is difficult to imagine anything other than an exclusive residential development and an equally exclusive marina. Token concessions to the historical might be expected to preserve a little character for the development but its authentic maritime industry seems lost forever.

The once busy wharves of Walsh Bay have already been leased for 99 years to Transfield for redevelopment as hotels, apartments and cultural facilities. The Woolloomooloo finger wharf, the largest of its type on earth, remains idle.

Home ownership is the Great Australian Dream, even if it's no longer the birthright it once was imagined. Protection of the value and environs of the family home, plus the ever-spiralling cost of harbourside real estate, mitigate against desperately needed new waterfront launching ramps and associated parking areas. Improvements to boat sheds, marinas, yacht clubs, indeed any marine facilities, especially those of an industrial scale, are resisted, often implacably.

Residents are suspicious of new developments, fear the traffic they might attract, and deplore the noise and apparent untidiness of the traditional waterfront. Mostly, however, they fear de-

valuation of their own investment, and there's the rub. Fears, expressed at the turn of the century that the harbour would become "a pond in a private paddock" seem increasingly prophetic. Yet marine facilities offer priceless access and services to boating Sydneysiders from near and far. Handled sensibly, they create the maritime character of the traditional waterfront that has always drawn the artist's eye.

The tension between the needs of the boating enthusiast, the rights of residents and the ambitions of (reasonable) developers, leaves Sydney harbour with pitifully few launching ramps, a dwindling number of boatsheds and arguably insufficient marine facilities — even fuel!

Compounding this trend is its abandonment by heavy marine industry (Cockatoo Island was the merely the most dramatic), the growth of Botany as an alternative container terminal, and a reduced presence by the navy and Sydney Harbour seems much closer to that "...pond in a private paddock". And an increasingly exclusive, isolated pond.

This is not to suggest that the jewel that is Sydney Harbour is losing its lustre. It is just that its maritime hues are diminished, which is a matter of taste for the beholder. The jewel itself, of course, remains priceless.

Many of the new Mediterranean-style town house developments west of the bridge, once weathered a little, will enhance the shorescape. Near derelict boatsheds have been spruced-up and marinas improved. And one cannot imagine buildings like Blues Point Towers ever being built along harbour shores again. And harbourside industry is not only on the wane, it is ruthlessly monitored for hints of pollution by governments and environmental activists.

The noblest gift to Sydney Harbour was round-the-world yachts-

Sydney Harbour jetcat ferry, 30 knots.

THE PORT

Sydney Harbour remains a busy seaport though its commercial shipping movements are diminishing.

Sydney Ports includes Sydney Harbour and the Port of Botany. Its collective turnover is growing but the Botany Bay terminal is steadily increasing its share of shipping, particularly its two dedicated container berths and a state of the art bulk liquids berth.

More than 75 shipping lines link Sydney Ports with 200 international destinations. It remains Australia's largest port in terms of total tonnage, though Melbourne was regarded a slightly larger container port in 1995-1996.

If the pendulum has swung towards Botany Bay, Sydney Harbour remains active. Some 900 cargo vessels still call into Sydney Harbour itself each year (compared with nearly 3000 in 1964-5) and 25 passenger vessels make an average of 75 visits a year between them.

Darling Harbour and White Bay have a number of berths that can handle various types of cargo as well as containers. Glebe Island remains the destination for the motor vehicle import trade. These facilities, plus the dedicated cruise terminals of Darling Harbour and the Overseas Passenger Terminal at Circular Quay, will help ensure that Sydney Harbour continues to play a significant role in commercial shipping well into the next millennium.

A luxury of the harbour's two passenger terminals is that they deliver the liners to the city's doorstep. Few passenger terminals in the world could compare with Circular Quay. New arrivals have the Opera House abeam, the Harbour Bridge overhead and the city before them — a splendid front door to Australia.

The twin ports of Sydney and Botany rank about 45th in the world. Ports of comparable tonnage are Southampton (UK), Barcelona (Spain), Savannah, Georgia (USA).

---

man Ian Kiernan's voluntary cleanup programme. It not only made a difference, it shamed the wider community, and jolted governments, confronting us with a grotesque reality. Sadly, the garbage and syringes find their way back, but if you cruise the harbour, the improvement is palpable. And the cleanup programme is ongoing.

Stormwater drainage into the harbour is surely the next great task. After heavy rains, the harbour is not only muddy and cluttered with flotsam, which is to be expected, it is also foul.

It is not enough that the quality of the harbour's waters is infintely better than most comparable international ports. The stewardship of such a rare natural gift demands the *highest* standards — and ruthless vigilance. The urban pressures upon it can only increase.

Ferries of all shapes and sizes ply the waterways, from the fast jetcats with speeds of 30 knots to the traditional ferries of more stately speeds. They shift some 13 million Sydneysiders a year lucky enough to start and end their working days with a soothing harbour trip. Once a year the ferries strut their stuff in The Great Ferry Race, a thunderous gala occasion and the choice for our cover picture.

During the week it's a working harbour as befits the nation's major port. On weekends its belongs to the boating public when hundred of yachts hoist flogging mainsails and slip their moorings and powerboats gurgle out to cruise or to fish its waters. Those who prefer the more familiar security of the shoreline can look.

And just looking is pleasure enough.

The view west from Darling Point across Rushcutters Bay, Wooloomooloo Bay, Farm Cove, the city and the upper harbour.

A BRIEF HISTORY

ON May 6, 1770, some eight days after having landed in Botany Bay during his voyage of discovery along the east coast of Australia, the great navigator Lieutenant James Cook, R.N. sailed past the entrance to Sydney Harbour, headed north. Though "two or three miles" out to sea, he spotted the entrance and intuitively noted in his journal that (his ship was) "...abreast of a Bay or a Harbour wherein there appeared to be safe anchorage which I called Port Jackson [for Sir George Jackson, one of the Secretaries of the Admiralty]." Though he did not enter the harbour, it was the first recorded sighting by a European. Nearly 18 years were to pass before its extent was known.

The loss of its American colonies in 1776, which denied the British Government a place of exile for its convicts, was among the chief reasons for establishing a colony in New South Wales, though knowledge of the region relied entirely on Cook's expedition. When the First Fleet of 11 ships — including nine chartered merchant vessels laden with convicts and stores, and two escort vessels, HMS *Sirius* and HMS *Supply* — arrived at Botany Bay after its 21,000-kilometre voyage, they were bitterly disappointed with its meagre freshwater sources and the in-hospitable mangroves of the shoreline. Captain Arthur Phillip R.N., who was in command of the expedition and was to become the colony's first governor, led a flotilla of three pinnaces

(open boats with sails and oars) to examine Port Jackson.

Thus the first Europeans entered the harbour. The official dispatch that recorded their joy and wonder has been quoted ever since:

> *Here all regrets arising from the former disappointment* [of Botany Bay] *was at once obliterated and Governor Phillip had the satisfaction to find one of the finest harbours in the world, in which a thousand sail of the line might ride in perfect security.*

When HMS *Supply,* commanded by Lieutenant Ball entered the harbour on January 25, she was the first ocean-going vessel to enter the harbour and maritime history. She anchored overnight in Sydney Cove to await the rest of the fleet.

Sydney harbour's first admirers were effusive. Their recorded comments include:

> *Port Jackson, I believe to be, without exception, the finest and most extensive harbour in the Universe, and at the same time the most secure, being safe from all winds that blow.*
>
> SURGEON-GENERAL JOHN WHITE

> *...this noble and capacious harbour, equal if not superior to any yet known in the world.*
>
> CAPTAIN COLLINS, MARINE

> *...a port superior, in extent and excellency, to all we had seen before.*
>
> CAPTAIN WATKIN TENCH, MARINE

THE HARBOUR ATTACKED

Guns were emplaced to defend Sydney Harbour at Fort Denison, Bradleys Head, South Head, North Head and Middle Head, and even Dawes Point, initially during the Crimean War. But none fired a shot in anger. The only action ever engaged in Sydney Harbour was on the night of May 31, 1942.

Three Japanese midget submarines entered the harbour, where Australian, British, American and Dutch warships were moored. The submarines were 24m long, with a crew of two and two torpedoes.

One was trapped in a submarine net at Sow and Pigs, its crew choosing *hara-kiri* rather than capture. Another fired two ineffectual torpedoes before being sunk. The third fired two torpedoes, one of which sunk the *SS Kattabul* off Garden Island, killing 20 sailors.

If their enthusiasm was influenced by gratitude and relief after a very long and dangerous sea voyage to an unknown land, plus the initial disappointment of Botany Bay, it was not the idle speculation of the ignorant. The First Fleet had called at another of the world's grandest ports, Rio de Janeiro, on the voyage out.

Captain Hunter, who led a party to chart the harbour while preparing sailing directions, apparently named Sow and Pigs, the rocky, partly submerged shoal that presents the only serious navigational hazard in the harbour. After passing it, so he observed, "...you may take what part of the channel you please, and anchor where you like."

Few harbours in the world could offer such unlimited latitude, especially in the days of sail.

Nearly 1000 people were landed at Sydney Cove, including officials, Marine guards and convicts. The two warships remained on station and the transports left. The tiny colony, with pathetically limited pioneering skills and a convict population with even less inclination to learn, eagerly awaited the Second Fleet and supplies. It did not arrive till June, 1790.

By January that year, Governor Phillip had a signal station — a flagstaff and hut — established at South Head, which was visible from the Observatory built on a high ledge at Dawes Point. Gunner Daniel Southwell, Master's Mate of HMS *Sirius*, had the lonely task of scanning the ocean for a sail. The signal flag was hoisted for the first time on February 10, announcing the return of HMS *Supply* from Norfolk Island. But on the evening of June 3, the signal flag flew again and to the wild delight of the colony: the *Lady Juliana*, the first of five vessels of the Second Fleet had been sighted. In fact it brought more convicts than supplies, many of whom were emaciated from scurvy and malnutrition. The First Fleet had been efficient, the second was a disgrace. Instead of relief, Governor Phillip found himself with another 1000 mouths to feed.

Nevertheless, the numbers of ships calling at Sydney Harbour gradually increased, including naval vessels, convict transports and storeships, mercantile trading vessels and whaling and sealing ships, both British and American. (First foreign vessel to enter the harbour was the American brig, *Philadelphia,* in 1792.)

During Governor Macquarie's term (1810-21) Sydney's population trebled to 30,000 with ever increasing numbers of free settlers. And in the New South Wales Gold Rush of the 1850s, the harbour sprouted a forest of masts as vessels from around the world converged on Sydney to deliver thousands of eager gold seekers. Sydney grew from 60,000 in 1850 to almost 400,000 in 1890. When the Gold Rush in New South Wales, and later Victoria, subsided, the growth of

Sydney and its harbour continued, along with the pace of the economy. It passed the one million mark in 1920.

After World War II, when the nation enjoyed one of the best standards of living on earth, the Australian government embarked on a massive European migration programme. This generated a steady stream of migrant ships entering Sydney Harbour, invariably the preferred Australian destination. It was the last great wave of the most distant migration in history.

The population of Sydney now exceeds 3 million and though migration continues — around 25 per cent of Sydneysiders are foreign born compared with 20 per cent of all Australians — most now come by air.

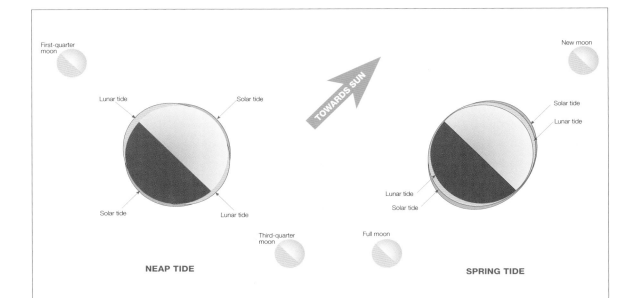

NEAP TIDE

SPRING TIDE

WHY TIDES HAPPEN?

The twice daily tidal rise and fall of the sea level is caused by the gravitational pull of the moon and sun, the moon having the bigger influence because it is so much closer.

When the moon is directly over a given point of the earth's surface — and thus exerts its maximum gravitational pull — the seawaters in that vicinity rise to a bulge in the direction of the moon. Water covering the earth on the opposite side of the earth — that body of water which is diametrically opposite and thus furthest from the moon — is also subject to this pull, and another bulge forms. At the crests of these two bulges, or waves, high water prevails; and because the volume of water is constant, low waters occur along the circumference of the earth perpendicular to the direct opposite tidal axis.

These low and high waters, called *lunar tides*, alternate in a continuous cycle as the moon circles the earth. At most shores around the world this happens twice a lunar day, which is 50 min. 28 sec. longer than the standard 24-hour day, (hence the timing of tides slipping a little each day). Successive lunar tides are generally about the same height, though in some areas they vary considerably.

Solar tides similarly give rise to an additional two oppositely-situated bulges or wave crests, though they are much shallower because the sun's gravitation pull is much weaker. (Despite its greater size, it is so much further away.)

The position of the lunar and solar tide crests depends on the positions of the moon and sun in relation to the earth. During new moons and full moons — when the sun, moon and earth are directly in line — the solar and lunar waves coincide to form one bigger than usual bulge, thus creating much higher and lower tides. These are called *spring tides* (*see diagram*), which are of obvious concern to the mariner. But when the moon is in its first or third quarter, the gravitational pull of both moon and sun reduce each other's influence, creating lower high-waters and higher low-waters. These are called *neap tides (see diagram)*.

The tide flowing inshore or upstream is a *flood tide*; the reverse is an *ebb tide*; and the period of reversal, when its influence is weakest, is called *slack tide*.

Sydney tides are calculated, in metres, from Fort Denison in the main harbour. Local tide charts are based on Eastern Standard time, with one hour added during Summer Time. Chart soundings, also shown in metres, indicate the depth at low water springs, in other words the worse case scenario.

SOME BASIC RULES

Here is a summary of basic rules for harbour users.

- When proceeding upstream, keep red marks to port (on your left) and green marks to starboard (your right). The opposite applies when heading downstream.

- Vessels approaching each other head-on must pass port to port (keep to the right: the *opposite* of road traffic).

- Overtaking vessels must keep clear of the overtaken vessel.

- Give way to the vessel on your starboard (right-hand) side (give way to the right).

- Always hold to the starboard side of a narrow channel (again, keep to the right).

- Give way to commercial vessels, particularly those flying a destination pennant and ferries displaying an orange diamond.

- Non-commercial power vessels give way to sail.

- As a matter of courtesy, cruising yachts should give room to racing yachts.

- Observe the speed limits of 4 knots (roughly, brisk walking speed) and 8 knots, displayed in black numerals on a yellow ground (shown below). No Wash Zones, require vessels to halt then proceed at a speed where no wash is produced. These limits are to protect other water users and the environment.

- Drink in moderation: if you are under the age of 18, the permissible alcoholic limit is 0.02; for 18 years and older, the limit is 0.05.

- In the event of an accident: stop; render assistance; exchange details; if someone is injured or the damage exceeds $100, report it to the Waterways or Water Police.

- All boats in New South Wales that are 5.5 metres or more, or capable of 10 knots or more, must be registered with the NSW Waterways. A period of three months' grace is given to visiting interstate vessels.

- For detailed information on boating requirements in NSW, telephone Waterways Authority on 13 12 36.

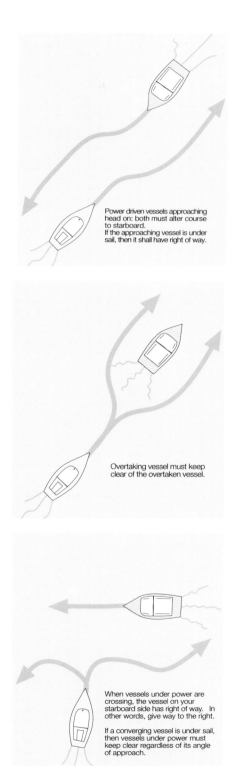

Power driven vessels approaching head on: both must alter course to starboard.
If the approaching vessel is under sail, then it shall have right of way.

Overtaking vessel must keep clear of the overtaken vessel.

When vessels under power are crossing, the vessel on your starboard side has right of way. In other words, give way to the right.

If a converging vessel is under sail, then vessels under power must keep clear regardless of its angle of approach.

NAVIGATION MARKS

Waterways are spending a great deal of money updating navigation marks in the harbour. There are two main types. Cardinal marks and lateral marks.

LATERAL MARKS

Lateral marks are easily identified by their red or green colour and their shape, though they appear in a variety of forms as shown below. They are simple to follow: Port hand marks are red and have a can-shaped topmark or buoy. They may or may not display a flashing red light. Keep these to your left when proceeding upstream. Starboard hand marks are green and have a cone-shaped topmark or buoy. They may or may not display a flashing green light. These should be kept to your right when proceeding upstream.

CARDINAL MARKS

Cardinal marks are more complicated. They mark foul ground such as reefs, rocks, mudbanks, etc that threaten navigation. Their shape and colour indicates which side you should pass to remain in deep water and keep clear of the hazard. To achieve this they are set in the compass quadrants. It is easiest to memorise the juxtaposition of the cones. The writer finds the following ditty helps remember the cones: *There's trouble up north, down south, out east and in the west.*

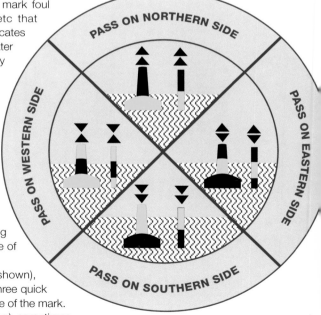

If the Northern quadrant is represented (as shown), sometimes with a white light displaying continuous quick flashes, you must pass on the northern side of the mark.

If the Southern quadrant is represented (as shown), sometimes with a white light displaying a series of six quick flashes followed by a long flash, then you must pass on the southern side of the mark.

If the Eastern quadrant is represented (as shown), sometimes with a light displaying a series of three quick flashes, then you must pass on the eastern side of the mark.

If the Western quadrant is represented (as shown), sometimes with a light displaying a series of nine quick flashes, then you must pass on the eastern side of the mark.

ANCHORING

To enjoy the many cruising spots discussed in the text, you need a reliable anchoring technique. Firstly, all craft should carry at least one anchor. The Australian Yachting Federation issues the following guide, based on either the length of the vessel or its displacement. The suggestions are minimums.

OVERALL LENGTH guide

| LOA | Anchor High holding power | | Chain | Warp | Suggested warp size | |
| | spade/ plough | Danforth | standard link | min. breaking force | polyethylene (silver) | nylon |
metres	kg	size	mm	kN	mm	mm
Under 5	3.5	4S	6	4.5	8	8
Up to 6	4	8S	6	9	10	10
Up to 8	7	13S	6	9	10	10
Up to 9	9	22S	8	20	16	12
Up to 11	11	22S	8	30	20	14
Up to 13	15	40S	10	39	24	16
Up to 15	20	65S	10	39	24	16
Up to 17	25	65S	13	45	26	18
Up to 19	34	80S	13	45	26	18

DISPLACEMENT guide

kilograms	Anchor High holding power spade/plough	Chain standard link	Warp min. breaking force	Suggested warp size polyethylene (silver)	nylon
less than 815	4	6	9	10	10
816 — 2500	7	6	9	10	10
2501—4300	9	8	20	16	12
4301 — 6550	11	8	30	20	14
6551 — 9500	16	10	39	24	16
9501 — 13600	20	10	39	24	16
13601 — 20400	25	13	45	26	18
20401 — 27200	34	14	45	26	18
27201 and more 45	14	60	32	20	

Choose your anchorage carefully, even for a lunch stop, but particularly if you plan to stay overnight.

- Will you have sufficient depth at low tide?
- Are there submarine cables in the vicinity? (If you accidentally jag a cable, cut your warp.)
- Will the boat obstruct a navigation channel, access route, moorings or buoys?
- Gauge your swing in tide or wind. Don't assume adjacent boats will swing at your speed.
- Lay anchor and chain on deck (check that the bitter end of the warp is attached to the boat!).
- Approach your chosen spot with minimum way, turning head-to-wind till the boat stops; as it begins to drift astern, lower the anchor, hand-over-hand; pay out cable to at least 3 times the depth of water; when the anchor grabs, cleat off, then take two bearings to check for drag.
- If all seems secure, you may gently reverse to help bury the anchor, and/or pay out more cable — up to seven times the depth of water if it is rough!

Your are trying to avoid: circling more than five times during the approach; anchoring so close to your neighbours you can hear what they're muttering; bumping on the bottom half way through an excellent lunch; losing anchor and warp over the side while watched by children; adjusting your line every other minute because you've wedged yourself in too close; irritating, or worse, amusing, the neighbouring boats.

The distinctive Hornsby Light at South Head, with Middle Head about 1 kilometre beyond it. The breaking water is South Reef, an extension of South Head. Approach the entrance midway between North and South Head and you'll have plenty of searoom. Many a racing yacht has scraped its keel cutting it too fine at South Head.

This chartlet describing the lights at the entrance, including the sectors beamed from Grotto Point is for explanatory purposes only. Vessels entering the harbour should refer to Royal Australian Navy Chart *Aus 200*.

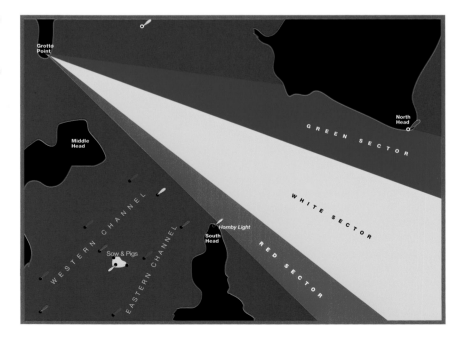

Grotto Point

North Head

GREEN SECTOR

Middle Head

WHITE SECTOR

WESTERN CHANNEL

Sow & Pigs

Hornby Light

South Head

RED SECTOR

EASTERN CHANNEL

THE ENTRANCE

*T*HE ENTRANCE to Sydney Harbour is 25 nautical miles (45 kilometres) north of Port Hacking and 10.5 nautical miles (19 kilometres) north of Botany Bay. The distance to Pittwater is 15 nautical miles north, or 27 kilometres, from South Head to Barrenjoey Head.

The entrance, readily identified in fair visibility, is flanked by the imposing sentinels of North Head and South Head — and a stirring sight for the homecoming sailor.

[Vessels proposing to enter the harbour, especially by night, should refer to Admiralty Chart *Aus 200*. This book is *not* intended as a substitute for proper navigational practice.]

NORTH HEAD

North Head is the more prominent, its sheer sandstone cliffs, crumbled rubble at their foot, rise some 70 metres above sea level. The North Head light on the cliff top marks the entrance, flashing a green isophase signal at 2 second intervals, which is visible from 3 nautical miles. ["Isophase" means that the duration of light and darkness is equal.]

SOUTH HEAD

South Head marks the southern side of the ocean entrance. This promontory's sheer sandstone cliffs rise from 20 fathoms or more to around 60 metres above sea level. South Head terminates in the lower peninsula of Inner South Head, a short underwater extension of which is South Reef — the only hazard in the 1.5 kilometre-wide entrance. The distinctively striped Hornsby

Light stands at the tip of Inner South Head, its long-flashing white light (5 seconds duration) visible from 15 nautical miles.

A further navigation aid is the Grotto Point light, clearly visible in a harbour approach. Its weakest colour can be seen for 9 nautical miles. It displays different colours, depending on what sector you are in during your approach: red if you are too close to North Head; white if you are in the fairway; and green if you are too close to South Head.

The ideal heading is 294 degrees, at which point you can line-up the white light of Grotto with a flashing green light (3 seconds), set well behind and just above it. (This light is mounted on the heights past Chinaman's Beach.)

If the North and South Head escarpments facing the ocean rise steeply from the deep to be pounded incessantly by Pacific swells, the lee shores of these great bulwarks slope to a string of protected sandy coves and beaches. Once inside South Head your are in flat water. Instantly. You have to sail further behind North head, which is not quite so benign, but you'll be well-protected.

In fact, ocean swells are experienced only at the harbour entrance and across The Sound, before dissipating at the broad mouth of Middle Harbour. However, in extreme conditions, swells crossing The Sound can rise steeply as they meet the shallower floor of Hunters Bay, breaking at Middle Head and Grotto Point, along the Balgowlah Heights foreshore and at the Gowlland Bombora.

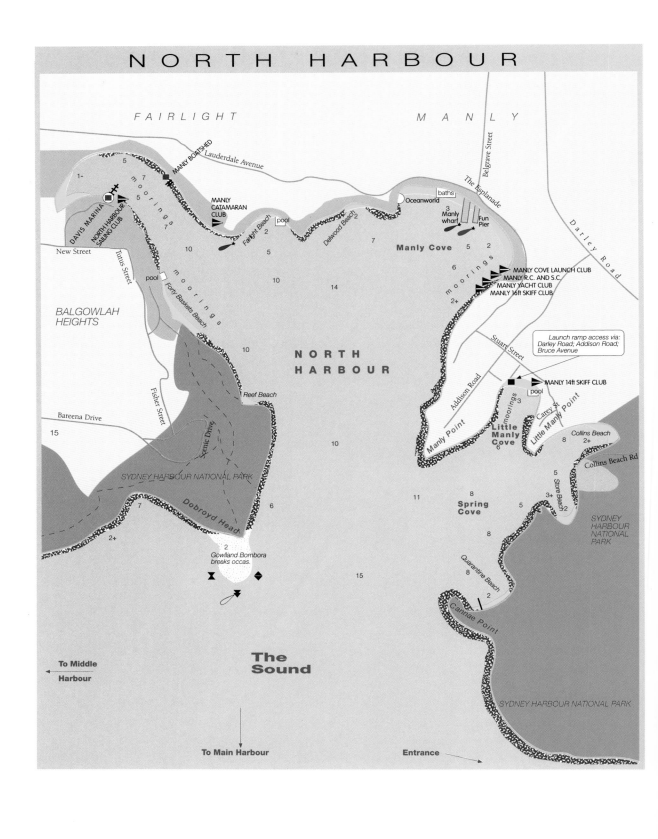

FAIRLIGHT

MANLY

MANLY BOATSHED

Lauderdale Avenue

Belgrave Street

The Esplanade

baths

Oceanworld

Darley Road

DAVIS MARINA

NORTH HARBOUR SAILING CLUB

5

7

5

moorings

7

MANLY CATAMARAN CLUB

Fairlight Beach

pool

2

5

Delwood Beach

2

7

3

Manly wharf

Fun Pier

New Street

Tittus Street

10

moorings

pool

Forty Baskets Beach

10

5

10

14

Manly Cove

5

2

6

moorings

2+

MANLY COVE LAUNCH CLUB
MANLY R.C. AND S.C.
MANLY YACHT CLUB
MANLY 16ft SKIFF CLUB

BALGOWLAH HEIGHTS

Fisher Street

Bareena Drive

15

Scenic Drive

10

Reef Beach

**N O R T H
H A R B O U R**

Stuart Street

Addison Road

Launch ramp access via:
Darley Road; Addison Road;
Bruce Avenue

MANLY 14ft SKIFF CLUB
pool

3

moorings

Carey St

Manly Point

Little Manly Point

Collins Beach

2+

SYDNEY HARBOUR NATIONAL PARK

Dobroyd Head

6

10

7

2+

2

*Gowlland Bombora
breaks occas.*

15

11

**Little
Manly
Cove**

6

**Spring
Cove**

8

8

5

8

5

3+

Store Beach

2

Collins Beach Rd

*SYDNEY
HARBOUR
NATIONAL
PARK*

Quarantine Beach

8

2

Cannae Point

**The
Sound**

To Middle
Harbour

To Main Harbour

Entrance

SYDNEY HARBOUR NATIONAL PARK

NORTH HARBOUR

FUEL : "NORTH HARBOUR"
PUBLIC LAUNCHING RAMP : LITTLE MANLY COVE

NORTH HARBOUR is the smallest arm of the harbour, though a broad body of water of good depth, with some inviting sandy beaches, a few of which are somewhat protected and pleasantly secluded. Its nearness to the entrance makes it a convenient first stop for cruising visitors, though its better anchorages are likely to be crowded at the height of summer, particularly on weekends.

North Harbour extends north from Cannae Point, which is tucked in the lee of North Head, just inside the entrance. Its northern shores are defined by the low lying Manly isthmus. The eastern shoreline is shaped by the rising cliffs of the Sydney Harbour National Park headland below Balgowla Heights, as far as Dobroyd Head. It opens onto The Sound, a deep trough in the harbour floor just inside the entrance.

The jaws of North Harbour are part of the Sydney Harbour National Park. The head falls within the municipality of Manly, a popular sea-

GOWLLAND BOMBORA

One of very few hazardous spots on Sydney Harbour, the Gowlland Bombora stands at the southernmost opening to North Harbour. It is an underwater ledge, extending in a southerly direction from Dobroyd Head. The area is clearly indicated with cardinal marks — flashing white light on its most southern extension — for good reason. Its waters can be deceptively untroubled in calm conditions but will break when a southeast swell is running. It can be dangerous in a southerly.

side resort and high-density residential area. Manly takes its name from observations by the colony's first governor who led a flotilla of three open boats to explore Port Jackson after the First Fleet's disappointment with Botany Bay.

Though no precise account of their movements survives, they were certainly in North Harbour between January 21 and 23, of 1788. Governor Phillip recorded: "The boats, in passing near a point of land in the harbour, were seen by a number of (Aboriginal) men, and twenty of them waded into the water unarmed...their con-

- ◼ MARINA WITH FUEL
- ◼ MARINA
- ◼ LAUNCHING RAMP
- ▶ YACHT CLUB
- ▢ RECREATIONAL AREA
- ▢ STATE/NATIONAL PARKS
- ▢ SAND, USUALLY MUDDY
- ▦ ROCKS
- 〜 MAJOR ROAD ACCESS
- ◣ STARBOARD NAV LIGHT/BEACON
- ◢ P ORT NAV LIGHT/BEACON
- ◁ WHITE/YELLOW NAV LIGHT/BEACON
- 4k MAXIMUM SPEED 4 KNOTS

fidence and manly behaviour made me give the name of Manly Cove to this place."

SPRING COVE

Spring Cove, the first irregular bay inside the steep cliffs of North Head, embraces four small coves [see Quarantine Beach, Store Beach, Collins Beach and Little Manly Cove]. There are no marks or lights to direct you, nor are they necessary. A vessel need only follow the headland in a northerly direction when entering the harbour to arrive at Cannae Point, the extremity of which is a small rocky islet with a 10-metre white flagmast clearly mounted at its peak.

The more northerly tip of Spring Cove — Manly Point — is readily identified by a prominent white, cylindrical block of units, ten storeys high.

Spring Cove has a sandy bottom, making it ideal for holding, with 2 to 5 metres depth as close as 30 metres from the shoreline. It is relatively protected from summer sea breezes but in the calmest conditions some surge must be

expected, generated by swell entering the heads, and the wash of passing vessels, particularly ferries.

Always lively in a southerly, it can churn like a washing machine if the southerly pipes, though its two most southerly coves, Quarantine and Store Beach, offer some protection, while not guaranteeing comfort.

QUARANTINE BEACH

This pleasant stretch of sandy beach is tucked behind the rocky projection of Cannae Point.

At the time of writing, no less than 11 signs in 100-odd metres forbid one thing or another: visitors must anchors at least 30 metres off the beach; no stern lines may be run to the beach; the area is out of bounds between sunset and sunrise; the Quarantine Station, an historic site beyond the beach, part of the Sydney Harbour National Park, may not be visited without prior arrangement; you may not moor alongside the jetty; only portable gas fires may be lit. Notwithstanding the overbearing officiousness of this

Quarantine Beach, the first cove inside North Head.

The most popular anchorage in North Harbour — Store Beach, Spring Cove.

number of signs — all reasonable enough regulations in themselves — it remains a delightful spot to anchor for a picnic or a swim.

If you keep the prescribed 30 metres offshore, you should have sufficient water beneath you, but if your draft exceeds 2 metres then you'll have to stand off a little further, where there is adequate depth. And though power vessels are forbidden to beach there, you can run a dinghy ashore or use the jetty to drop-off or collect passengers.

The Quarantine Station (above the beach) was gazetted in 1838 so that smallpox and typhus victims — even bubonic plague victims — could be isolated. Various "fevers" found their way to the colony, almost from the outset of transportation. Smallpox, and particularly measles, ravaged the aborigines around the harbour. As early as April, 1789, Lieutenant Bradley RN, of HMS *Sirius,* reported: "From the great number of dead natives found in every part of the harbour, it ap-

pears that the small pox had made dreadful havoc among them." (Historians believe this may have been measles, from which the aborigines had no immunity).

The *Constitution,* out of Southampton in 1855, had 49 cases of smallpox on board when it arrived. A further 11 eventually died at Quarantine. During Sydney's smallpox plague of 1881, 178 people were shipped to Quarantine; and of 302 victims quarantined during the bubonic plague of 1900, 90 died there.

The station's last significant function was much kinder: billeting survivors of Cyclone Tracy, which devastated Darwin in the Northern Territory at Christmas, 1974.

Long closed, the Quarantine Station is now a protected historic site, where tombstone epitaphs can only hint at the depth of lonely suffering endured there. The area is controlled by the National Parks and Wildlife, through which visits can be arranged.

Store Beach

This beach, tucked under the steep slopes of the southern headland, is the most snug, the most charming, and hence the most popular of the four coves. Much the same rules apply — 30 metres offshore; no stern lines to shore [see Quarantine Beach] but the beach and its wooded surrounds, plus the excellent protection, makes this one of the most popular weekend anchorages on Sydney Harbour. Don't expect privacy at the height of summer. It will be packed tight. But on weekdays or during winter, this is a sublime, isolated anchorage. There are no facilities ashore, but Little Manly Cove (see entry) is only about 500 metres away. Alternatively, hardier souls can climb to the walking track to link up with Collins Beach Road, but it is a fair hike into to Manly.

Collins Beach

Anchoring is forbidden in this snug little cove, north of Store Beach. Warning signs are displayed either side of its entrance, though landing is permitted. This is less of a disappointment than it might seem, because the waters in this cove shoal sharply.

LITTLE MANLY COVE

Little Manly Cove has advantages if not the protection and relative isolation of the other inlets of Spring Cove. It is completely developed, with a park on the eastern point, a sandy beach at its head, behind which is a grassed area, and beyond that, the roadway (Stuart Street). There are toilets and a kiosk behind the beach and a netted swimming area in the eastern corner. In the northern corner is a concrete boat ramp — the only one in the whole of North Harbour! The rocky northwestern shore is lined with houses to the water's edge.

The cove is extremely exposed to southerlies (and to be avoided if it is a strong one) but comfortable enough in summer sea breezes. What it does offer is access to shore facilities. There are moorings in most of the cove but it has a good sandy bottom for holding, a soft beach for landing a dinghy, and a street that will lead you to shops — or in to Manly if you are up to the hike.

MANLY COVE

This is the hub of North Harbour activity, the focal point of which is the Manly-Circular Quay ferry terminal, which must be given a wide berth. The activity creates plenty of movement, and the area is crowded with moorings and sailing clubs.

It does, however, offer instant access to shops and restaurants of all kinds, various recreational pursuits, and public transport, via the main beach (anchor at the eastern end, off the baths), Delwood Beach or Fairlight Beach. Oceanworld aquarium, east of the Manly baths, may be of particularly interest to boating visitors. The fun fair is likely to tempt the kids. The continual slop at Manly Cove and along the northern shoreline of North Harbour precludes any real comfort at anchor, though the ground is secure enough. A strip of public park along the shore offers a handy and decidedly more stable alternative for the family picnic.

"NORTH HARBOUR"

This small cove in the northwest corner of North Harbour is what locals often refer to as "North Harbour". It seems odd that such a significant cove has never been officially named. The cove shoals to mudflats at its head, beyond which is a small park. The only handy shop is near the southeast corner of the park.

The Manly Boatshed, which has been owned by the well-known Treharne sailing family since the 1940s, stands on the northern shore, offering a slipway with 4 cradles (maximum 20 tons) repairs, detailing and rigging.

In the southeastern corner is Davis Marina, which carries both diesel and petrol fuel, ice and cold drinks. It also offers casual day/night moorings to visitors, plus toilet and shower facilities.

Visitors should pull alongside the fuelling wharf. Davis Marina carries out a wide range of marine services and its twin slipways are large enough to haul out vessels up to 80 feet or 40 tonnes.

Anchoring is impractical because of the density of the moorings.

Forty Baskets Beach

There is invariably some movement here, though it is less crowded with moorings than nearby "North Harbour". It offers a pleasant outlook, a sandy beach with baths at the northern end.

Reef Beach

Tucked into rocky promontory of Dobroyd Head, this tiny, isolated beach, is now — after long and acrimonious debate — no longer designated a nudist beach. The decision puts this delightful picnic spot firmly back on the list of worthwhile North Harbour destinations for recreational sailors. It is not recommended for an overnight stay because of the movement but it is certainly worth a visit. Ashore, you can link-up with the pleasant tracks through the Sydney Harbour National Park network .

MIDDLE HARBOUR

FUEL : THE SPIT, SAILORS BAY, ROSEVILLE
RAMPS : ROSEVILLE, TUNKS PARK

◉   MARINA WITH FUEL
◼   MARINA
◼   LAUNCHING RAMP
▶   YACHT CLUB
☐   RECREATIONAL AREA
☐   STATE/NATIONAL PARKS
☐   SAND, USUALLY MUDDY
▦   ROCKS
◁   MAJOR ROAD ACCESS
◁   STARBOARD NAV LIGHT/BEACON
◁   PORT NAV LIGHT/BEACON
◁   WHITE/YELLOW NAV LIGHT/BEACON
4k   MAXIMUM SPEED 4 KNOTS

*M*IDDLE HARBOUR, which opens on to The Sound, westward of the entrance, offers variety, protection and relative freedom from commercial harbour traffic. Its broadest waters are near its mouth, in Hunters Bay, between the promontories of Grotto Point and Middle Head. Its busy hub is The Spit, where the waters narrow to a small lifting bridge, beyond which is Inner Middle Harbour, a mixed canvas of waterside suburbia and fiord-like wooded vistas. Further upstream, the waters eventually narrow again to the meanders of Middle Harbour Creek.

Hunters Bay offers inviting harbour beaches at its head and relatively protected sailing courses, particularly for dinghies. The busier Spit offers more beaches, marine facilities, yacht clubs and moorings. Inner Middle Harbour, with its flat, deep waters, about half of which are cloaked with bushland reserves, is a cruising sanctuary where solitude and even communion with the sounds of the bush can be experienced if you know when and where to look — though less likely on summer weekends!

Middle Harbour's one great limitation is the bottleneck at its hub: The Spit Bridge, with a closed height of only 5.1 metres, opens only at fixed times. Recurring dreams for a suitably high bridge to allow unimpeded navigation are periodically aired, then quietly shelved. Only suicidal yachties should hold their breath awaiting a practical solution. Meanwhile, there are reasons to be grateful for the *status quo*. The bridge opens regularly (see chart) and reasonably often, given its critical road traffic function. After all, how many major cities on earth would deliberately choke a major northern traffic artery to a standstill so that a solitary yacht, engaged in nothing more pressing than private pleasure, might pass? It's a consoling thought if you happen to miss the last bridge for the night, if somewhat lost on those

Grotto Point lighthouse, viewed from the entrance. Note the rocky southern extension, much of which is submerged at high tides. Keep well clear, especially in a heavy swell, when breaking waves will rise.

OUTER MIDDLE HARBOUR

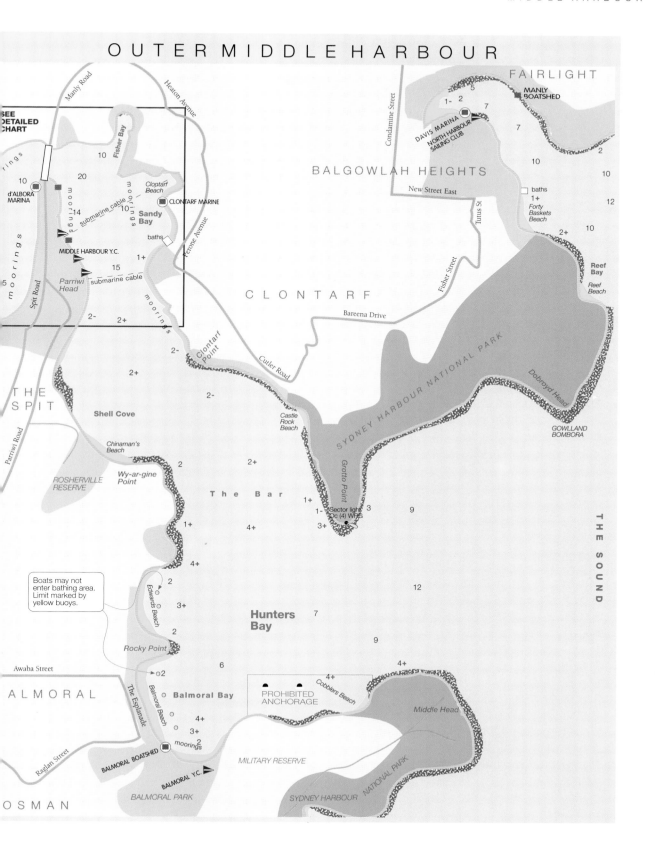

FAIRLIGHT

Manly Road

Heaton Avenue

SEE DETAILED CHART

Fisher Bay

moorings

10

20

14

10

d'ALBORA MARINA

moorings

submarine cable

Cloptarf Beach

CLONTARF MARINE

Sandy Bay

baths

10

MIDDLE HARBOUR Y.C.

15

submarine cable

1+

Parriwi Head

Spit Road

moorings

2-

2+

Condamine Street

MANLY BOATSHED

1- 2

7

DAVIS MARINA

NORTH HARBOUR SAILING CLUB

5

BALGOWLAH HEIGHTS

New Street East

Tutus St

10

7

2

baths

1+

Forty Baskets Beach

2+

10

10

12

Reef Bay

Reef Beach

Fisher Street

CLONTARF

Bareena Drive

Clontarf Point

2-

2+

Cutler Road

SYDNEY HARBOUR NATIONAL PARK

Dobroyd Head

GOWLLAND BOMBORA

THE SPIT

Parriwi Road

Shell Cove

Chinaman's Beach

Wy-ar-gine Point

ROSHERVILLE RESERVE

2+

2

Castle Rock Beach

The Bar

Grotto Point

1+

1-

3+

Sector light
Oc (4) WRG

3

3

9

THE SOUND

1+

4+

4+

Boats may not enter bathing area. Limit marked by yellow buoys.

Edwards Beach

3+

2

12

Hunters Bay

7

9

Rocky Point

Awaba Street

2

6

ALMORAL

The Esplanade

Balmoral Beach

Balmoral Bay

4+

Cobblers Beach

4+

PROHIBITED ANCHORAGE

Middle Head

4+

4+

3+

moorings

2

BALMORAL BOATSHED

Raglan Street

BALMORAL Y.C.

MILITARY RESERVE

SYDNEY HARBOUR NATIONAL PARK

OSMAN

BALMORAL PARK

Sydneysiders who have never known the frustrations of having to lower their masts.

GROTTO POINT

Grotto Point, with its prominent lighthouse, marks the northerly entrance to Middle Harbour. Its rocky foot extends in a southerly direction just beneath the surface, causing a short natural break in any sort of swell. In extreme conditions it can generate waves big enough to attract surfboard riders. It is best given a generous berth in any weather — at least 70 metres off the point.

Inside the point, the rocky foreshore is broken by a couple of tiny sandy beaches, most notably Castle Rock Beach. However, the waters inside a line between Grotto Point and Clontarf Point are very shallow, though usually flat because of the protection of the headland.

THE BAR

The Bar is a broad sand bar that extends from the eastern shores — between Grotto Point and Clontarf Point — right across to the western shores along the rocky headland of Wy-ar-gine Point, the shallowest parts being some 2.5 metres, though a midstream heading offers safer depths, the shallowest sections of The Bar being between Grotto Point and Clontarf Point.

MIDDLE HEAD

The southernmost point of Outer Middle Harbour is marked by the steep cliffs of Middle Head, which bear the brunt of the sea swell that enters through the heads, though much of its venom is dissipated by the depths of The Sound.

There is good depth quite close to the rocks but it is best given a wide berth to avoid the incoming swells and a backwash spiteful enough on mild days to upend everything below deck that is not secured. Particular caution should be exercised off the most westerly point of these heads, where waves can break occasionally close-in in otherwise mild conditions.

In 1824, the square rigger *Edward Lombe,* out of London, struck Middle Head at night. Twelve perished, including the Captain, Second Mate and Third Mate. Middle Head also claimed the Aberdeen clipper, *Catherine Adamson,* in 1857, a harbour pilot among those lost when she was swept on to the rocks and capsized.

If a heavy swell is running, particularly after sustained offshore storms, then boats entering Middle Harbour are advised to keep midway between Grotto Point and Middle Head, because the swells between the two points can be steep enough to break at both ends, if rarely.

Cobblers Beach

This tiny beach in a rocky amphitheatre is tucked in behind the protective wall of Middle Head. There's a pleasing little park there surrounded by wooded slopes. If your sensibilities preclude nude sunbathing, however, this may not be the bay for you. In any event, anchoring is not permitted here, being part of the naval waters that extend along the foreshore of HMAS *Penguin*.

HMAS Penguin

The large brick buildings of *HMAS Penguin* on Middle Head completely dominate the southern slopes of Hunters Bay, beneath which is a marine complex of wharves, workboats and moorings, that are out of bounds to the public.

The military is to vacate Middle Head and an impassioned battle is presently being waged at State and Federal level to prevent the land from being sold for development. Some even hope that the area will be cleared and returned to bushland as a logical extension·to the adjoining Sydney Harbour National Park.

Balmoral Beach

The head of Hunters Bay is dominated by the sweeping sandy ribbon of Balmoral Beach, the most popular, not to mention the most fashionable, of harbour beaches. It is really three connected beaches. The southern segment of the beach has a maritime flavour with moorings and

Looking east across Outer Middle Harbour, from Parriwi Head, towards Grotto Point (left) and the more distant Middle Head. Nearer (right) is Whyargine Point, with the delightful Chinaman's Beach tucked inside.

the Balmoral Boatshed, where fuel, bait, a small slipway, moorings and hire boats are available. A park behind the beach is partially screened from the water by splendidly shady fig trees at the water's edge. In the eastern corner of the park is the Balmoral Sailing Club, a small family sailing club that sponsors a number of popular dinghy classes.

Balmoral baths divide this segment of the beach from the long stretch of sand that is the main bathing beach.

Boats should note that a string of buoys off the beach mark the offshore limits, inside which navigation is forbidden. The beach is for swimmers only, though it's pleasant to anchor offshore, beaching your dinghy at the eastern end.

A particular attraction for the boating fraternity — and Balmoral Beach has an array of sensory distractions at the height of summer — is the number of shops, including a chemist, fast food outlets and restaurants along The Esplanade, which extends the length of the beach.

Right: The Bathers Pavilion, Edwards Beach. Awaba Road in the background leads to Spit Road, Balmoral.

Edwards Beach

A rocky islet, connected to the shore by a small pedestrian bridge, divides Edwards Beach from its better known neighbour, Balmoral Beach. Edwards is the setting for The Bathers Pavilion, an elegant white landmark that is the most significant and obvious building in Hunters Bay. It is has long been a very popular quality restaurant. Shark-proof netting strung across the southern corner of the beach offers a protected swimming area. Offshore buoys mark the approach limit for boats.

Chinamans Beach

This exquisite sandy bay is largely protected by the steep slopes of Wh-ar-gine Point to the east, which is dominated by modern homes. This is one of the best beaches on the harbour, enhanced by a pleasant park behind it that has water and public toilets. It's a long, steep walk up the hill to Spit Road and shops, so unless you need particular provisions, it's easier to motor a kilometre or so to The Spit.

Holding ground off the beach is excellent and though Chinamans can be a little rocky in a northeaster, it is rarely uncomfortably so. Its access to Spit Road and the Spit, plus the very pleasant outlook, makes it an ideal Middle Harbour anchorage.

THE SPIT

The bottleneck of the Spit is the maritime hub of Middle Harbour. Though its name is derived from the sand spit that extends from the suburban slopes of Balmoral/Beauty Point down to The Spit Bridge, the term is used to embrace the adjacent waters across to the eastern shores of Clontarf. It is a 4-knot zone.

Though the Spit offers ready access to The Spit Road, deep water, and good holding ground, anchoring is difficult because of crowded moorings and the need for a clear navigation channel, particularly near the bridge. Nevertheless, a temporary spot can usually be found off the eastern shore (the Spit side is too busy and too crowded) and sandy beaches on both sides of the narrows make landing a dinghy agreeable.

Below: Middle Harbour Yacht Club at the Spit.

⬤	MARINA WITH FUEL
⬛	MARINA
⬛	LAUNCHING RAMP
▶	YACHT CLUB
⬜	RECREATIONAL AREA
⬜	STATE/NATIONAL PARKS
⬜	SAND, USUALLY MUDDY
▦	ROCKS
～	MAJOR ROAD ACCESS
◗	STARBOARD NAV LIGHT/BEACON
◖	PORT NAV LIGHT/BEACON
◯	WHITE/YELLOW NAV LIGHT/BEA...
4k	MAXIMUM SPEED 4 KNOTS

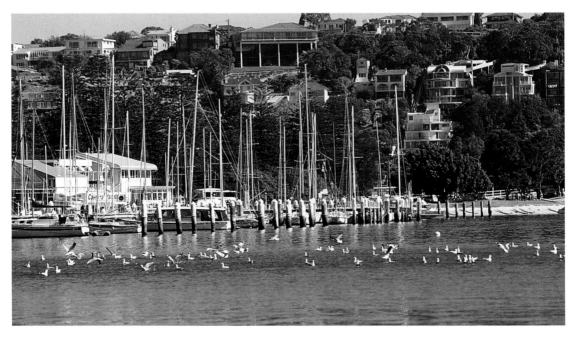

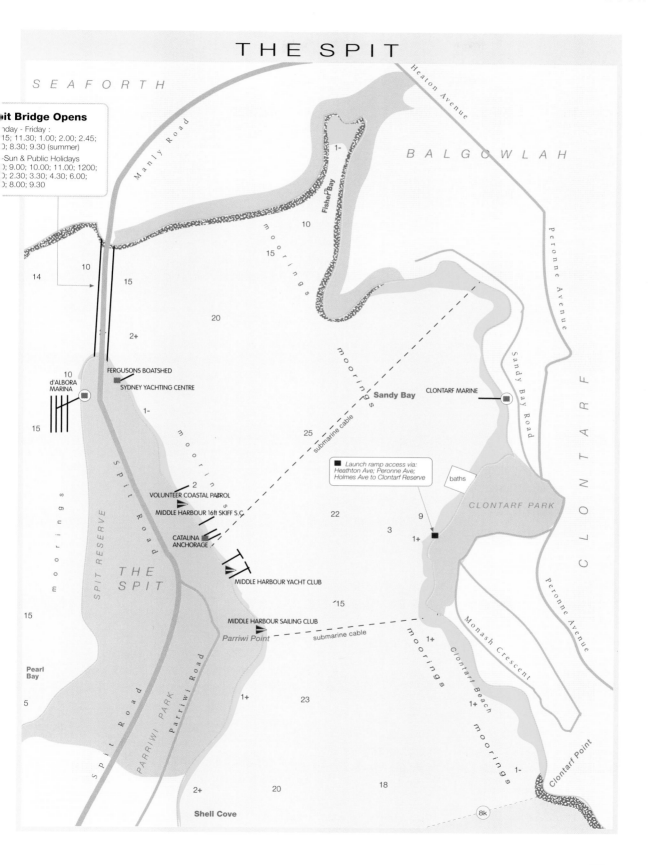

THE SPIT

SEAFORTH

BALGOWLAH

Spit Bridge Opens

...nday - Friday :
...15; 11.30; 1.00; 2.00; 2.45;
...0) 8.30; 9.30 (summer)
...Sun & Public Holidays
...0) 9.00; 10.00; 11.00; 1200;
...0) 2.30; 3.30; 4.30; 6.00;
...0) 8.00; 9.30

Heaton Avenue

Manly Road

Fisher Bay

Peronne Avenue

10

15

moorings

14

10

15

20

2+

moorings

Sandy Bay Road

10
d'ALBORA
MARINA

FERGUSONS BOATSHED

SYDNEY YACHTING CENTRE

Sandy Bay

CLONTARF MARINE

CLONTARF

15

1-

moorings

25

submarine cable

baths

■ Launch ramp access via:
Heathton Ave; Peronne Ave;
Holmes Ave to Clontarf Reserve

CLONTARF PARK

SPIT RESERVE

Spit Road

moorings

2

VOLUNTEER COASTAL PATROL

MIDDLE HARBOUR 16ft SKIFF S.C.

22

9

3

1+

CATALINA
ANCHORAGE

THE
SPIT

moorings

15

MIDDLE HARBOUR YACHT CLUB

Peronne Avenue

15

MIDDLE HARBOUR SAILING CLUB

Parriwi Point

submarine cable

1+

Monash Crescent

moorings

Clontarf Beach

Pearl
Bay

Parriwi Road

PARRIWI PARK

Parriwi Road

1+

23

1+

Spit Road

5

2+

20

18

moorings

1-

Clontarf Point

Shell Cove

8k

The Spit offers an abundance of marine services, restaurants and access to regular bus services, but precious little in the way of shops for provisioning. Fuel is available at Clontarf Marina on the eastern side of the bridge and at d'Albora Marina on the western side.

Fergusons Boatshed is nearest the bridge on the eastern shores. It has a marine electrician, trimmer, divers and a slipway (up to 30 tonnes). Adjacent is the Sydney Yachting Centre, with a chandlery, which also provides cool drinks, a canoe sales/hire outlet, a brokerage and the Northside Sailing School. Visitors by boat are advised to land their dinghy on the adjacent beach.

Further south is the Volunteer Coastal Patrol, the Middle Harbour 16ft Skiff Club and the Catalina Anchorage, which has a slipway, shipwrights and a brokerage.

The Middle Harbour Yacht Club, inside Parriwi Head, offers excellent facilities to members and their guests.

Clontarf Beach

This popular beach, opposite the Spit, stretches from Clontarf Point along the eastern shores and around Clontarf Park.

Temporary anchoring is possible just beyond the line of moorings, particularly at the Clontarf Point end. Clontarf Marine is prominent in the cove at the northern end of the beach, which is particularly crowded with moorings.

Clontarf Marine has both marine berths and moorings, slipways that can accommodate 15 tonnes (yachts) and 20 tonnes (power boats). It has shipwright, engineering, trimming, rigging and gas fitting services. Most important to passing vessels, it has fuel, both diesel and petrol.

FISHER BAY

This tiny cove, the last before the Spit bridge, is

The Spit Bridge, viewed from downstream.

crowded with moorings but it is sometimes possible to anchor at the mouth or to pick up one of two emergency mooring buoys at the mouth while awaiting a bridge opening.

THE SPIT BRIDGE

The centre section of the bridge, 5.1 metres above the water and some 24 metres wide, is raised at regular intervals (see charts for times). Opening times, *which are altered in the winter/summer seasons*, are posted on both sides of the bridge. A warning bell is sounded when the road traffic grates are raised and traffic lights on both sides are switched on to alert boats minutes before the bridge is raised.

Traffic through the bridge can be crowded, particularly on race days, including large sightseeing ferries. Don't assume your fellow travellers either know the rules or care. (You occasionally see boats jump the gun to anticipate the green light, steaming through the narrow opening to the consternation of right-of-way boats pouring through from the opposite direction!)

Boats awaiting the opening should congregate on the starboard side of the waterway (so that boats passing through the bridge from the opposite direction have a clear navigation path); be under power (not sail); and await the green light. Consideration for the banked-up road traffic suggests that movement should be urgent, but orderly. An occasional hazard is the wash of large power boats, reduced to displacement speeds, pushing up a big wash — so don't pass too close to the walls of the opening if you don't wish to snag your rigging when you rock and roll.

Willoughby Bay, near the head of Long Bay, Inner Middle Harbour.

Unmasted vessels might note that the fixed span to the north of the opening is higher than the lifting segment, offering 6.4 metres headway.

INNER MIDDLE HARBOUR

A seamanlike tip: before leaving the bridge behind you, note the opening times (and the time you came through) so at to better time your homeward run.

Only one thing spoils a blissful day in Inner Middle Harbour more than a frantic rush for the bridge, the diesel smoking, all on board sunburnt and, perhaps one or two tired-and-emotional — and that's watching the bridge lowered as you

approach! The bridge operators are remarkably obliging but they have their duty.

PEARL BAY

This is the first (southern) bay past the Spit Bridge, tucked in behind d'Albora Marine and particularly well-protected from a southerly by Beauty Point. There are moorings here — and the only permanent houseboats in Sydney harbour! There is room to anchor beyond the moorings, keeping well clear of the marina. Shore access, despite the seawall, is easy enough through The Spit Reserve, which follows the shoreline around Beauty Point to Quakers Hat.

The d'Albora Marine dominates this side of The Spit with its 200-odd marina berths. It is a major marine complex within which a number of separate business operate, including a chandlery, a brokerage, a restaurant and kiosk. Marine services include a slipways (maximum load 50 feet or 25 tonne); full mechanical services from outboards upwards; shipwright services; fuel, both diesel and petrol; and a free waste pump-out station.

The reach between Seaforth and Beauty Point is otherwise pleasant, though unremarkable, with houses and moorings lining the steep Seaforth

Pretty Salt Pan Cove, sometimes called Wreck Bay.

shores. Beyond this you can alter course southward for Long Bay, proceed (almost) directly west into Sailors Bay, or northward for the very best of Inner Middle Harbour cruising.

LONG BAY

Long Bay is the southwest extension of Inner Middle Harbour, a delightful reach within which are situated the small coves of Quakers Hat Bay, Willoughby Bay and Salt Pan Cove. The easterly shores of Long Bay are lined with waterside homes and moorings, though there's room for anchoring. Where to land to advantage is more problematical. The western shores are preferable, and more picturesque, where most of the green cover is part of the Northbridge Golf Course.

At the head of Long Bay is Tunks Park, with the only public launching ramp in the area. Cammeray Marina commands the gentle waters at the head, a popular destination for overseas and interstate cruisers. (Note: it is a 4-knot zone past Folly Point.) It has repair facilities, a brokerage, and two slipways (maximum 20 metres LOA or 40 tonnes), swing moorings and pens. You can buy ice and LPG but not fuel.

WILLOUGHBY BAY

Arguably the prettiest little cove in the vicinity, Willoughby Bay is well protected from the elements by its steep, wooded banks. This is a 4 knot zone. There are few houses beyond Folly Point, which marks its northern entrance. At the (southern) head of the bay is Primrose Park, which should be approached with caution. The mud shallows extends some 60 metres from the seawall. Moorings make anchorage all but impossible, most of which are controlled by Lyons Boatshed, tucked into the western banks of the bay, which has a slipway, shipwright services and a small brokerage.

SALT PAN COVE

This charming, shallow little cove (sometimes called Wreck Bay) is surrounded by thickly-wooded slopes but spoiled by a broken-backed

steel wreck that discourages access. There is, nevertheless, a little good water south of the wreck but it shoals suddenly at the second part of the wreck, which can be submerged at high tide. Some will undoubtedly claim the wreck has historical significance but if this rusting hulk is monumental, it is monumental junk that diminishes this beautiful corner of Long Bay.

QUAKERS HAT BAY

The first cove inside Long Bay, Quakers Hat Bay is picturesque but crowded with moorings and, overlooked by homes at the water's edge on all but the point. Tom Joel's Boatshed (small pontoon to come alongside) offers a few day-moorings, bait, water and hire boats and two small slips (12 metres LOA). But the future of this little boatshed was put in doubt after a fire in July, 1997.

Mr Joel (87), moved to the bay in 1927 with the family boat-building business, which had built the first boatshed at The Spit (1900) before moving via Balmoral to Quakers Hat. The ashes of the July fire were barely cold before developers were making offers. Time will tell if yet another quaint little harbour boatshed is lost.

SAILORS BAY

Sailors Bay is probably the busiest in Inner Middle Harbour and the density of moorings makes it an extremely doubtful choice for cruising. Public access, though, is easy enough: through Clive Park on the southern headland; Sailors Bay Park on Mowbray Point; and a strip of reserve along the northern shores.

Northbridge Sailing Club commands the mouth of the bay, followed by the small Sailors Bay Boatshed and slipway, which offers repairs, a small slipway and a brokerage.

The head of the bay is dominated by the public

⬤	MARINA WITH FUEL
■	MARINA
■	LAUNCHING RAMP
➤	YACHT CLUB
▢	RECREATIONAL AREA
▢	STATE/NATIONAL PARKS
▢	SAND, USUALLY MUDDY
▦	ROCKS
〜	MAJOR ROAD ACCESS
◆➤	STARBOARD NAV LIGHT/BEACON
◆➤	PORT NAV LIGHT/BEACON
◇➤	WHITE/YELLOW NAV LIGHT/BEACO
4k	MAXIMUM SPEED 4 KNOTS

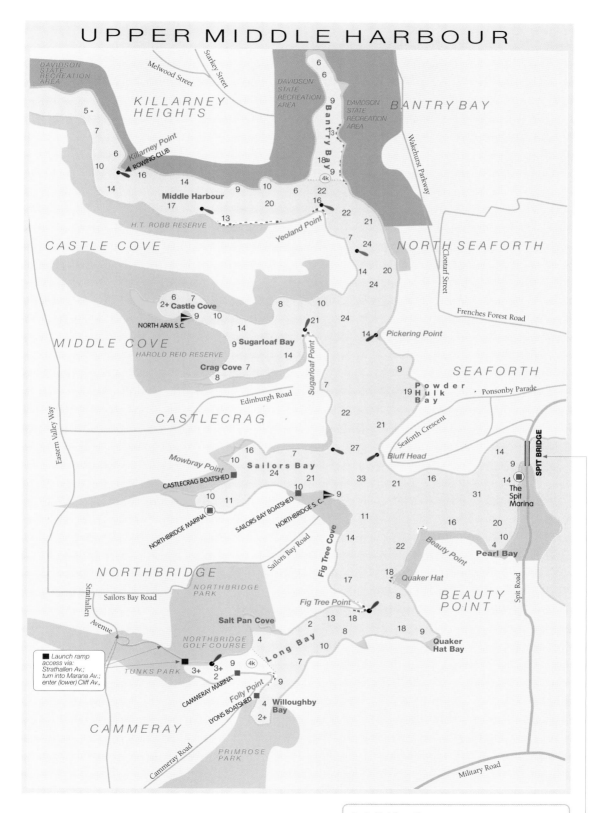

UPPER MIDDLE HARBOUR

DAVIDSON STATE RECREATION AREA

Melwood Street

Starkey Street

KILLARNEY HEIGHTS

DAVIDSON STATE RECREATION AREA

BANTRY BAY

Bantry Bay

DAVIDSON STATE RECREATION AREA

Wakehurst Parkway

5 -
7
6
10
Killarney Point
ROWING CLUB
14
16
14
Middle Harbour
17
20
13
H.T. ROBB RESERVE
9
10
6
16
22
22
21
Yeoland Point
7
24
14
20
24

9
3
18
9
(4k)

NORTH SEAFORTH

Clontarf Street

Frenches Forest Road

CASTLE COVE

6
7
2+ Castle Cove
9
10
NORTH ARM S.C.
14
Sugarloaf Bay
9
14
Crag Cove 7
8

8
10
21
24
14
Pickering Point

9

SEAFORTH

MIDDLE COVE

HAROLD REID RESERVE

Sugarloaf Point

7

Edinburgh Road

22

Powder Hulk Bay
19
Ponsonby Parade

Eastern Valley Way

CASTLECRAG

21
Seaforth Crescent

16
Mowbray Point
10
Sailors Bay
24
CASTLECRAG BOATSHED

7
27
Bluff Head

33
21
16

SPIT BRIDGE

14
9
14
The Spit Marina
31

10
11
NORTHBRIDGE MARINA

10
SAILORS BAY BOATSHED
9
NORTHBRIDGE S.C.
21

11

Fig Tree Cove

16
20
10
4
Pearl Bay

NORTHBRIDGE

NORTHBRIDGE PARK

14
22
Beauty Point

Sailors Bay Road

Fig Tree Point

18
Quaker Hat

8
BEAUTY POINT

Spit Road

Strathallen Avenue

Sailors Bay Road

Salt Pan Cove

NORTHBRIDGE GOLF COURSE
4
Long Bay
2
13
18
8
17

18
9
Quaker Hat Bay

Launch ramp access via: Strathallen Av.; turn into Marana Av.; enter (lower) Cliff Av.,

TUNKS PARK
3+
3+
2
9
(4k)
7
10
9

CAMMERAY MARINA
Folly Point
LYONS BOATSHED
4
Willoughby Bay
2+

CAMMERAY

Cammeray Road

PRIMROSE PARK

Military Road

Spit Bridge Opens
Monday - Friday :
10.15; 11.30; 1.00; 2.00; 2.45; 7.30; 8.30; 9.30 (summer)
Sat-Sun & Public Holidays
8.00; 9.00; 10.00; 11.00; 1200; 1.00; 2.30; 3.30;
4.30; 6.00; 7.00; 8.00; 9.30

The ideal protected anchorage at the head of Castle Cove, Sugarloaf Bay.

POWDERHULK BAY

Beyond the steep slopes of The Bluff, to which homes of the well-to-do cling like fabricated barnacles for the excellent views, lies Powderhulk Bay. Unremark-remarkable when compared with more northerly bays, it is fairly crowded with moorings.

SURGARLOAF BAY

Houses dot the escarpment of Sugarloaf Point, though the southern waterfront, which has private moorings along its length, has a narrow fringe of public reserve. The high slopes that protect the rest of the bay are part of large bushland reserves. There is room to anchor in the bay but the best of it is in two coves that fork off at its head, either side of the Harold Reid Reserve bluff — Crag Cove and Castle Cove. (When referring to Sugarloaf Bay, many invariably mean Castle Cove.)

CRAG COVE

Often called the South Arm, this is a pleasant alternative when the more popular Castle Cove is crowded. The water shoals sharply to mud flats at the head. Useful visual bearings are a prominent rock outcrop about half way into the cove on the northern shore and a pink-coloured cottage on the southern shore: if you keep to the bay side of an imaginary line between these two points you will have around 2 metres beneath you, and considerably more the further you stand off. Stray inside the line and you're in trouble.

The bottom is good holding mud.

baths and Northbridge Marina, whose many moorings include unusual strings of fore-and-aft moorings. Its slips can handle vessels around 26 tonnes. It does not sell fuel.

Castlecrag Marine stands on Mowbray Point, off Sailors Bay Park, which also offers a small brokerage and slipway. Its moorings extend for a considerable distance off the point into the bay.

NORTHERN ARM

INNER MIDDLE HARBOUR

As you head north along the northern arm of Inner Middle Harbour, the vista before you rivals any on the harbour. On a misty morning, or in a rain squall, it evokes a fiord-like grandeur and mood. Beyond The Bluff and Pickering Point (on the eastern shores), and beyond Sugarloaf Point to the west, the wooded slopes of the western promontory plunge from the heights of Castle Cove to the distant narrows, the steep slopes of North Seaforth marking the opposite shores.

Beyond these narrows rise more wooded folds, forming a bushland sanctuary, dense enough to screen the waterway from North Shore suburbia. This makes it one of the most tranquil and treasured cruising destinations on Sydney Harbour.

◉	MARINA WITH FUEL
■	MARINA
■	LAUNCHING RAMP
➤	YACHT CLUB
□	RECREATIONAL AREA
□	STATE/NATIONAL PARKS
□	SAND, USUALLY MUDDY
▦	ROCKS
～	MAJOR ROAD ACCESS
➤	STARBOARD NAV LIGHT/BEACON
➤	PORT NAV LIGHT/BEACON
➤	WHITE/YELLOW NAV LIGHT/BEACON
4k	MAXIMUM SPEED 4 KNOTS

BANTRY BAY & SUGARLOAF BAY

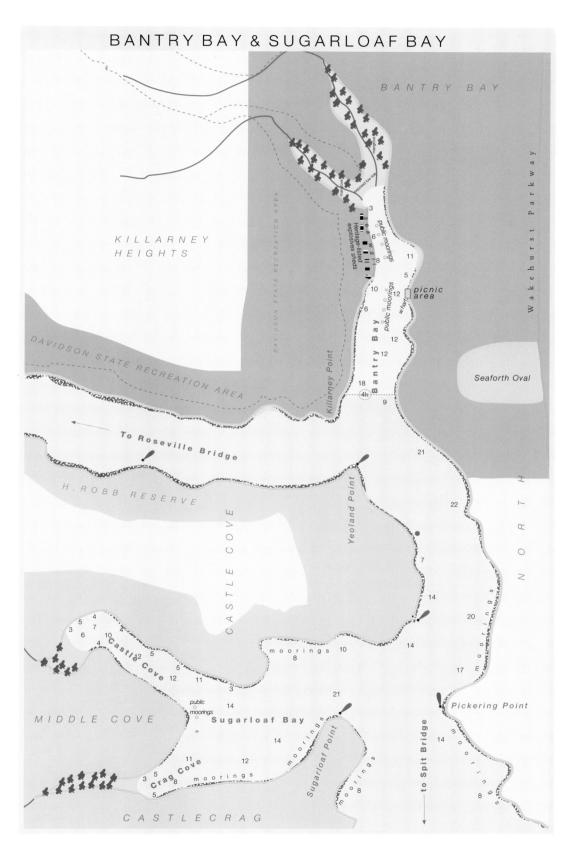

BANTRY BAY

KILLARNEY HEIGHTS

DAVIDSON STATE RECREATION AREA

DAVIDSON STATE RECREATION AREA

Wakehurst Parkway

Heritage-listed explosives sheds

public moorings

public moorings

wharf

picnic area

Seaforth Oval

Killarney Point

Bantry Bay

NORTH

To Roseville Bridge

H. ROBB RESERVE

CASTLE COVE

Yeoland Point

CASTLE COVE

moorings

Castle Cove

MIDDLE COVE

public moorings

Sugarloaf Bay

Crag Cove

moorings

Sugarloaf Point

moorings

moorings

Pickering Point

to Spit Bridge

CASTLECRAG

Bantry Bay, looking towards the head from the picnic terrace. The brick buildings on the opposite shore are the old explosives stores.

There are some excellent bush walks around the bluff which connect to Rembrandt Drive in Middle Cove.

CASTLE COVE

Often called the North Arm, this deep little cove, protected by wooded slopes, is the most secluded and the most popular inlet in Sugarloaf Bay. Nevertheless, on weekdays or during winter, it is possible to find solitude here. (If you attract the curiosity of a few wild ducks in the vicinity, all have developed a Pavlovian expectation of being fed when boats visit.) There is good depth in most of the cove but it does shoal to mangrove mudflats at the head (see chart), so keep well clear. The perfect anchorage, in the writer's view, is near the north banks at the head of the cove (*see* photo p40).

BANTRY BAY

Once past Sugarloaf Bay, the waterway narrows, then divides. Head westward to Roseville Chase and Middle Harbour Creek; due north for Bantry Bay. Bantry Bay and Sugarloaf Bay are Middle Harbour's most popular cruising destinations. The former is totally isolated from suburbia by the surrounding Davidson Park State Recreation Area.

The only development there is the string of brick explosives magazines, abandoned in 1974 after 57 years. Hidden behind the brick facades, the stores are tunnelled into the hillside, their timber floors spark proof — no nails or screws! These abandoned buildings are "heritage listed" but out of bounds to the public. Vessels may not come alongside the sea wall, let alone put crew ashore there. (Explosives were first stored in hulks in Bantry Bay, after having been removed from the Goat Island when is was converted to a bacterialogical station to combat Sydney's bubonic plague outbreak in 1900.)

MARINA WITH FUEL
MARINA
LAUNCHING RAMP
YACHT CLUB
RECREATIONAL AREA
STATE/NATIONAL PARKS
SAND, USUALLY MUDDY
ROCKS
MAJOR ROAD ACCESS
STARBOARD NAV LIGHT/BEACON
PORT NAV LIGHT/BEACON
WHITE/YELLOW NAV LIGHT/BEACO
4k MAXIMUM SPEED 4 KNOTS

MIDDLE HARBOUR CREEK

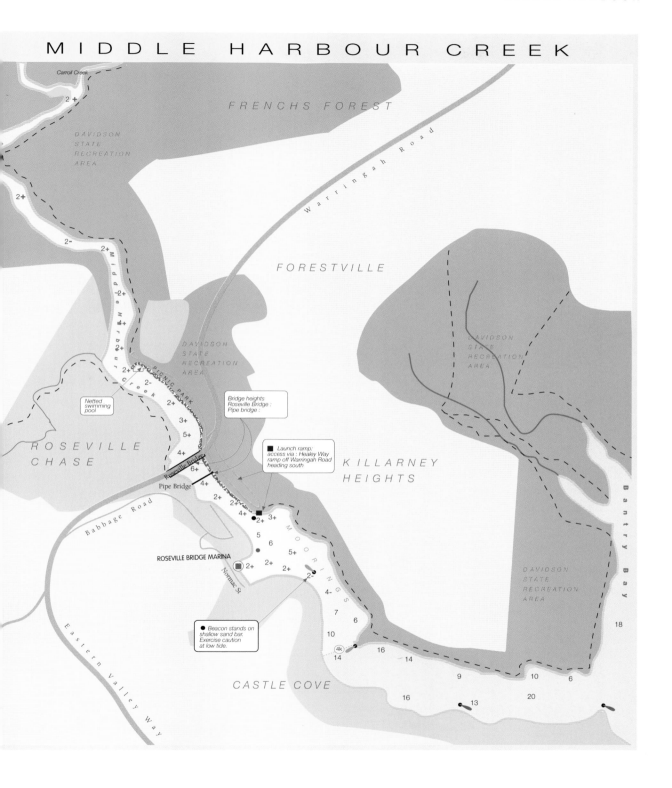

Carroll Creek

2+

FRENCHS FOREST

DAVIDSON
STATE
RECREATION
AREA

Warringah Road

2+

FORESTVILLE

2+

Middle Harbour Creek

2+

2+

DAVIDSON
STATE
RECREATION
AREA

2+

DAVIDSON
STATE
RECREATION
AREA

Netted
swimming
pool

PICNIC PARK

2+

Bridge heights
Roseville Bridge :
Pipe bridge :

3+

5+

■ Launch ramp:
access via : Healey Way
ramp off Warringah Road
heading south

KILLARNEY
HEIGHTS

ROSEVILLE
CHASE

4+

Roseville Bridge

6+

Pipe Bridge

4+

2+

2+

4+

●■ 3+

Babbage Road

5

6

MOORINGS

5+

DAVIDSON
STATE
RECREATION
AREA

ROSEVILLE BRIDGE MARINA

■ 2+

2+

2+

Normac St

● Beacon stands on
shallow sand bar.
Exercise caution
at low tide.

4-

7

6

Bantry Bay

Eastern Valley Way

10

16

18

4k

14

16

14

9

10

6

CASTLE COVE

16

13

20

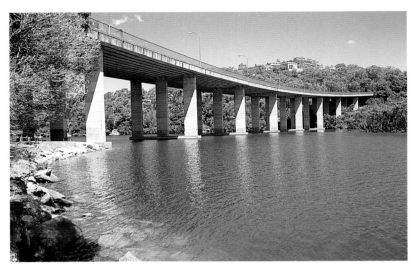

Roseville Bridge has 17.4 metres clearance but the downstream pipe bridge is much lower, with only 11 metres.

gift of the Davidson Park State Recreation Area, which stretches for more than 1200 hectares — from the head of Middle Harbour Creek in Frenchs Forest, along Killarney Heights, and completely enfolding Bantry Bay, and on to Seaforth.

Importantly, it protects the upstream catchment for the many tiny creeks that feed Middle Harbour Creek.

Its deep-wooded folds form a precious green barrier against the pressure of urban development. Most of it remains undisturbed bushland, apart from walking paths along the foreshores, which provide the only access. You don't have to walk far into this rugged bushland before the silence is broken only by birdsong and the occasional crackle of nervous wildlife scampering from your path for better litter cover. These reserves not only provide a sense of isolation along the upper Middle Harbour waterways, they create a mood of adventure.

On the eastern side of the bay there is a small jetty where you may put passengers ashore. An elevated picnic area behind the jetty, replete with tables, seats and a barbecues, offers both comfort and a splendid view of the bay (*see* p42).

There are 8 public moorings midstream, but ample room and comfortable depth to ride to anchor if these are occupied, provided you do not stray into the very head of the bay, which shoals suddenly to mangrove flats (beyond the northern end of the seawall on the western shore).

Closest road to Bantry Bay is the Wakehurst Parkway, about 20 minutes hike eastward along the walking track to Seaforth Oval.

Flat Rock Beach

There is a particularly charming little beach tucked into the tiny, rocky cove on the northern shore, just upstream from Bantry Bay. There can be unsettling movement from passing vessels but it's a pleasing outlook and adequate depth to anchor, provided you stand some 50 or more metres off the beach.

Davidson Recreation Area

The bushland along the northern shores of Upper Middle Harbour owes its preservation to the civic

ROSEVILLE CHASE

To follow upper Middle Harbour, turn west at Yeoland Point. These are pleasant cruising waters cloaked by bushland reserves, but this particular stretch — almost to Killarney Point — is best left to the waterskiers who ply it (relentlessly) on summer weekends. Upstream from Killarney Point, the waters become shallower. It is navigable, though deep-drafted vessels should proceed with caution to Echo Point; and beyond it, very carefully indeed.

The Roseville Bridge Marina, which nestles in a snug cove inside Echo Point, is the last point upstream to offer marine facilities. The waters here are well-protected but shallow. Depths of

Roseville Bridge Marina, tucked inside Echo Point, has excellent facilities and a tranquil location.

2-plus metres in the cove shoal to a clean sandy beach around Echo Point itself, a soft landing spot for dinghies. Above the beach is a picnic area with plenty of green shade on two levels — and drinking water taps. An underrated cruising destination in the harbour, the writer lived aboard his boat here for six idyllic months.

When approaching this cove (upstream), keep well clear of the starboard beacon marking its southernmost point: it sits on a small sand bar where the water shoals sharply to 1.5 metres and less, particularly on the northeastern side. If following the prescribed channel (that is, keeping the navigation mark to starboard), the water is deepest about midway between the mark and the shore. Be cautious: we are talking about 2 metres at low tide. Moorings on the opposite northeastern shore enjoy more than 3 metres, so deep-drafted vessels might skirt close to the moorings along that shore on the "wrong" starboard side of the navigation mark, turning sharply back to midstream when the marina is 90 degrees off the port bow.

A 4 knot zone, which applies to all navigable waters further upstream starts at the navigation mark. A submarine cable crosses the waterway at this point.

The Roseville Bridge Marina offers permanent berths and swing moorings (including day-only rates when available) a brokerage, and full marine services. Its three slips are capable of carrying up to 30 tons and 2.13 metres (7ft) draft. It has both diesel and petrol bowsers on the main jetty, sells ice, and has a cafe that serves breakfast and lunch at weekends in season.

If you need supplies, it's a long, steep climb to shops on the brow of the hill along Warringah Road. (The marina has plans for a inclinator up to the street level).

On the northeastern shore — opposite Echo Point — is a launching ramp, with an adjacent kiosk that opens in summer. All vehicles enter-

The surrounding slopes create a natural amphitheatre around the waters immediately upstream from the Roseville Bridge. A park (right) offers barbecue facilties, public toilets and water taps. Middle Harbour Creek narrows and becomes much shallower beyond this point.

ing the park on weekends, which includes those vehicles launching boats, are required to pay a small fee. There is a parking area behind the concrete launch ramp and a floating jetty alongside.

MIDDLE HARBOUR CREEK

If your draught is 2 metres or more, navigating beyond the Roseville Bridge is simply not worth the hassle. In any event, deep-draughted yachts are likely to be frustrated by the height of the pipe bridge (11 metres clearance only at high water springs) which spans Middle Harbour Creek some 50 metres downstream of the higher Roseville Bridge (clearance of 17.4 metres).

Beyond the bridge, the creek widens. Mangroves line the western shores but the broad green sward of picnic grounds stretch around the lazy bend of the eastern banks — a tiny cultivated section of the Davidson Park State Recreation Area, with vehicle access from Warringah Road. The picnic ground extends about a kilometre upstream to a sharp bend in the creek, where a small swimming net is set. Barbecue fireplaces are available for public use, fire bans permitting. The picnic ground, popular at weekends, is invariably deserted during the week — and, in the writer's experience, spotlessly maintained to complement this splendidly protected anchorage.

Launches and yachts with suitably shallow draft, say 1.5 metres, can worm their way upstream for about 3 kilometres to the fork that marks the confluence of Middle Harbour Creek and Carroll Creek. To find the deepest channel, cross and re-cross the creek to hug the steepest, rockiest banks, keeping well clear of the flatter banks, particularly those with mangroves.

Some, including the writer, find it well worth the effort, though the last two kilometres, if not all the waters above Roseville Bridge, are more practically explored in a dinghy. If your draft is 2 metres or more — and in the unlikely event you can clear the bridges — you could well find yourself aground.

And stranded!

THE LOWER HARBOUR

FUEL : ROSE BAY, DOUBLE BAY, RUSHCUTTERS BAY, MOSMAN BAY, NEUTRAL BAY
PUBLIC LAUNCHING RAMP : ROSE BAY

*F*OR the purposes of this book, the Lower Harbour is taken to mean all of Port Jackson that lies east of its most obvious landmark, the Sydney Harbour Bridge. All of the harbour west of the bridge, including the Parramatta River and Lane Cove River, is covered in the section called the Upper Harbour.

Harbour's tides tend to be ignored by all but racing yachts because they are so benign. They have a rise and fall of about 1.5 metres, and run at less than a knot in most parts, though this increases to around 1.5 knots at the entrance.

The Lower Harbour beaches are sandy, particularly those along its eastern shore. The harbour floor is mostly mud or sand, both of which provides good holding ground.

Certainly the Lower Harbour is busiest. It is the biggest and broadest body of water in the harbour and all shipping movements must pass through it, but it is the network of ferry services plus the commercial and recreational boating that creates the most activity. Activity means wash, so you must expect some joggle wherever you are in the lower harbour.

The entrance and The Sound are influenced by the ocean swells and can be threatening in heavy weather. But once inside South Head, or Middle Head, the waters flatten in the shelter of Lower Harbour. Parts of the harbour can become quite rough in a blow, with short, sharp wind waves, but if it's waters can become uncomfortable they are not treacherous. And at least temporary shelter is never more than a kilometre away, and rarely that far. One should, of course, never underestimate the elements in any large expanse of water: the harbour has taken its toll of ships and souls. Nevertheless, it is a very safe, sheltered harbour, provided you practice prudent seamanship.

THE SOW AND PIGS

The only serious impediment to navigation in Sydney Harbour is a reef known as Sow and Pigs, which is covered at high tide. At low tides, when its rocks are largely exposed, they are said to resemble a pig and her piglets, or so it apparently seemed to the early settlers who named them. (The writer, however, has yet to meet a soul who has recognised the resemblance!) The problem with these rocks is that they lie at the centre of the harbour fairway, which is otherwise unemcumbered. If you stretched a line from Inner South Head to Georges Head, Sow and Pigs would sit some 800 metres from each point.

The position of Sow and Pigs, however, is clearly indicated by five marks: it is pegged out by four cardinal, each indicating which side you should pass; and a more central mark, mounted on the reef itself, is a white-flashing beacon (6 seconds).

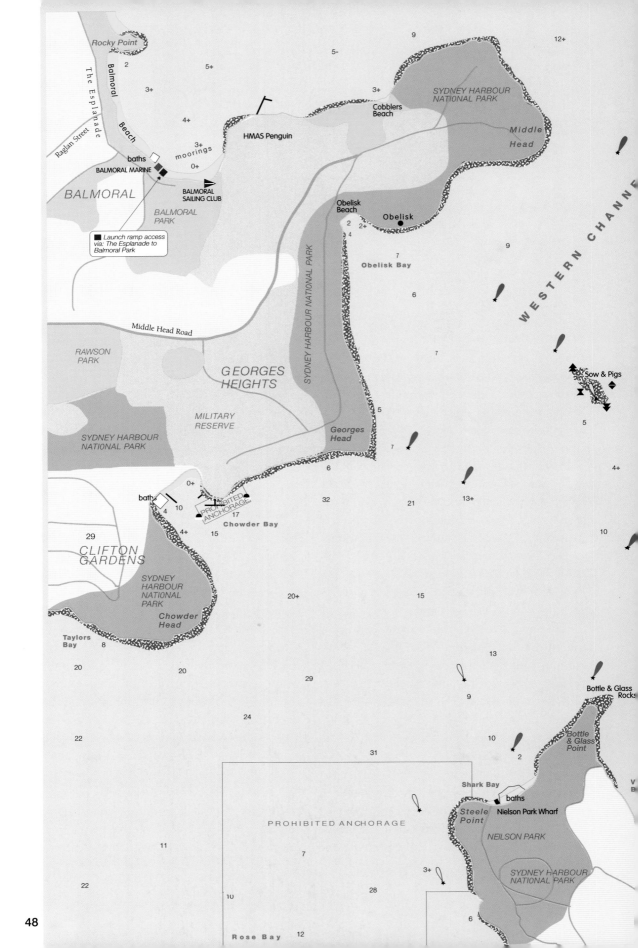

Rocky Point

2

The Esplanade

Balmoral Beach

Raglan Street

baths
BALMORAL MARINE

BALMORAL

BALMORAL PARK

3+

4+

3+
moorings

0+

BALMORAL SAILING CLUB

5+

5-

9

12+

HMAS Penguin

Cobblers Beach

3+

SYDNEY HARBOUR NATIONAL PARK

Middle Head

■ Launch ramp access via: The Esplanade to Balmoral Park

Obelisk Beach

2

4

2+

Obelisk

Obelisk Bay

7

9

6

SYDNEY HARBOUR NATIONAL PARK

Middle Head Road

RAWSON PARK

GEORGES HEIGHTS

MILITARY RESERVE

SYDNEY HARBOUR NATIONAL PARK

7

5

Georges Head

7

6

WESTERN CHANNEL

Sow & Pigs

5

5

4+

10

baths

0+

4

10

PROHIBITED ANCHORAGE

17

Chowder Bay

15

32

21

13+

29

CLIFTON GARDENS

4+

SYDNEY HARBOUR NATIONAL PARK

Chowder Head

20+

15

13

Taylors Bay

8

20

20

29

9

Bottle & Glass Rocks

24

22

10

2

Bottle & Glass Point

31

Shark Bay

baths

Steele Point

Nielson Park Wharf

NEILSON PARK

11

PROHIBITED ANCHORAGE

7

3+

SYDNEY HARBOUR NATIONAL PARK

22

10

28

6

Rose Bay

12

MIDDLE HEAD TO NIELSON PARK

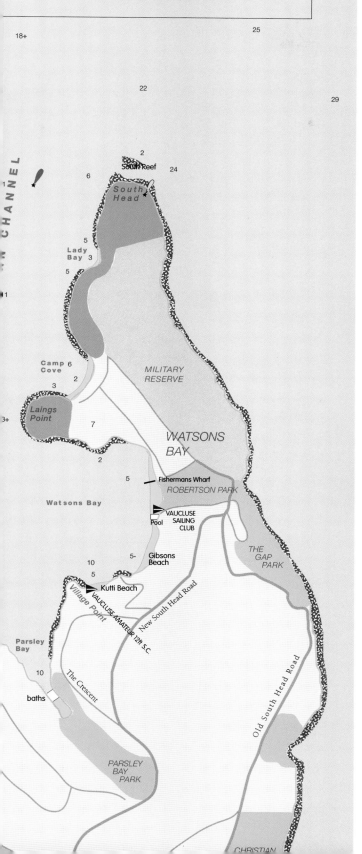

18+

25

22

29

2
South Reef   24

6

South
Head

5
Lady
Bay   3

5

Camp 6
Cove
2

3

Laings
Point

3+

7

MILITARY
RESERVE

WATSONS
BAY

2

2

5   Fishermans Wharf
ROBERTSON PARK

Watsons Bay

VAUCLUSE
SAILING
CLUB
Pool

5-   Gibsons
Beach   THE
GAP
PARK

10
5

Kutti Beach

VAUCLUSE AMATEUR 12ft S.C.

Village Point

New South Head Road

Parsley
Bay

10

The Crescent

baths

Old South Head Road

PARSLEY
BAY
PARK

CHRISTIAN

CHANNEL

1

1

MARINA WITH FUEL
MARINA
LAUNCHING RAMP
YACHT CLUB
RECREATIONAL AREA
STATE/NATIONAL PARKS
SAND, USUALLY MUDDY
ROCKS
MAJOR ROAD ACCESS
STARBOARD NAV LIGHT/BEACON
PORT NAV LIGHT/BEACON
WHITE/YELLOW NAV LIGHT/BEACON
4k   MAXIMUM SPEED 4 KNOTS

THE WEDDING CAKE

A quaint feature of Sydney Harbour is its two elegant white "Wedding Cakes" that light the upstream ends of the Eastern Channel (green) and the Western Channel (red), beyond Sow and Pigs. They might well be described as maritime Sydney's contribution to the charm of Australia's Federation Period of architecture, which at its authentic best was more than functional, yet neither too fussy nor grand. First built in 1912, the Wedding Cakes are largely timber, painted white and pleasingly proportioned. Undoubtedly they could be replaced with more "cost-efficient" structures but it would be a loss. Like Sydney's best lighthouses, they have an invaluable aesthetic and historical identity beyond function. And the Wedding Cakes still work.

In reality, the reef is all toq easily avoided and its sinister reputation quite undeserved. Certainly countless overeager (or ignorant) boating enthusiasts, particularly racing yachtsmen, may have damaged their keels on it. The writer once watched two innocent Americans hit it dead centre in a brand new J24 with every stitch of nylon aloft. And commercial shipping must surely have scraped it on occasion. Yet the only record of a substantial wreck on Sow and Pigs that the writer could find was that of the 600-ton *Phoenix* out of London in 1824! And even the *Phoenix* didn't sink, though the damage may have doomed her, because she disappeared with all hands on her next voyage, bound for Newcastle.

In any event, Sow and Pigs can be safely and more sensibly skirted by keeping to either side in the clearly marked Eastern or Western Channels. Both channels have port and starboard beacons to guide you along their fairways.

OBELISK BAY

This tiny rocky cove, tucked well in behind second fold in the cliffs on the south side of Middle Head, has the advantage of a bush setting that is part of the Sydney Harbour National Parks chain. It is also a nudist beach. If you don't find that discouraging, there is good depth in the approaches to the bay but once inside the protected point there is little room to manoeuvre, which can be made more difficult by the swell.

It should be approached with some caution, keeping well clear of the point upon which the obelisk is mounted. There is 8 metres of water abreast of this point; half way into the bay it reduces to 6 metres; and there is around 4 metres off the pylon marking the inner limits for vessels, all of which is of good holding sand.

Powerboats are prohibited from landing.

A path from the bay joins the excellent bush walk that stretches from Bradleys Head to Balmoral.

CHOWDER BAY

Chowder Bay is an underrated North Shore cruising destination. Though some movement must be expected, it can be remarkably comfortable, particularly if you tuck in close to Chowder Head and the shark-proof baths. Even if you prefer more room, the southern side of the bay is favoured, and with good depth to anchor. Waters around the public jetty which extends past the baths must the kept clear; similarly the Army Maritime School and its extensions on the northern headland. Naval waters extend from the northern shore.

The Sydney Harbour National Park extends around most of the bay, the balance of which is a Military Reserve. The Clifton Gardens park at the head of the bay has water taps and public toilets as well as a tidal swimming enclosure off the beach.

LADY BAY

The first rocky little cove inside Inner South Head, Lady Bay is probably better suited to its role as a designated nudist beach than as an anchorage. Often (incorrectly) called Lady Jane Beach, the water is invariably disturbed, a flow-on effect from swells at the nearby entrance, and passing harbour traffic. Four submarine cables in the vicinity makes the prospect of anchoring here even more problematic.

Above the bay stands the Royal Australian Navy establishment of HMAS *Watson*. A fringe of the Sydney Harbour National Park — which covers the tip of South Head — lies between the water and the Military reserve that is perched on the heights. The park offers an interesting walk and some spectacular views along the cliff tops.

A yellow spar buoy that is usually set off the bay is *not* a navigation mark. It is a turning mark for harbour yacht racing — a spot to be avoided on Saturday afternoons in summer, particularly if you have guests of some sensitivity aboard. Roundings there can be chaotic and the exchanges tend to a distinctly salty flavour.

CAMP COVE

Camp Cove is a site of historic moment. It was

the first landing place by Europeans in Sydney Harbour. The admirable Governor Phillip, leading boldly from the front in a completely unknown environment, commanded a flotilla of three pinnaces in search of a more promising site than Botany Bay had proved to be for the First Settlement. An obelisk in the park on Laings Point marks the event.

This is a 4-knot zone and vessels are forbidden to approach the beach here closer than the pylons (just offshore), which display warning signs marking the extent of the swimming area.

Boats anchoring in the cove must be manned at all times but depth is not a problem, with 3 to 4 metres at the pylons, deepening to 5-plus metres further out in the cove, and sandy holding ground. As with Lady Bay, a little movement must be expected, even on quiet days.

Camp Cove beach is an inviting sandy stretch for a swim or easy access to Victoria Street, Watsons Bay. There is also a track for a pleasant walk around the cliffs, past Lady Bay, to Sydney Harbour National Park at South Head.

WATSONS BAY

The first bay of size or consequence inside South Head is Watsons Bay, between Laings Point and Village Point. It was named for Robert Watson, of HMS *Sirius*, one of the early pilots on the harbour and Harbourmaster in 1811.

A tiny park is perched on the rocky extremity of Laings Point but private homes line the northern shores of the bay to the sandy beach at its head. Behind the beach is Doyles seafood restaurant, a popular Sydney icon. A hotel is adjacent.

The southern end of this strip of beach is dominated by a large jetty, known as Fishermans Wharf, which is shared by a seafood restaurant, the Sydney Game Fishing Club and a water taxi service. The extreme end of the jetty and its northern face are available to the public. Access, however, is rarely easy, particularly on weekend when the traffic can be very busy.

Robertson Park, which lies behind the jetty, has public toilets.

Anchoring in Watsons Bay isn't easy either. Navigation around the jetties at the head of the bay must be left unhindered — particularly around Fishermans Wharf and the Pilot Boat Base — and the bay itself is crowded with moorings.

The quickest solution is to anchor beyond the moorings, where the mud offers good holding, and accept a fair row to the beach if you need to go ashore.

The Pilot Boat Base stands in the southeast corner of the bay. In the early colonial period, ships entering the harbour would moor at Watsons Bay, awaiting harbour berths. North of the Pilot Boat Base is the public baths and the Vaucluse Yacht Club. The Vaucluse Amateur 12ft Sailing Club is situated between Gibsons and Kutti beaches.

PARSELY BAY

Parsley Bay is better protected and considerably less busy than Watsons Bay to its north. It is almost impossible to anchor close in because of the density of moorings. But there is deep water

Doyles seafood restaurant, Watsons Bay, a popular Sydney icon.

Vaucluse Bay, one of the prettiest developed bays on the harbour.

and good holding ground beyond the moorings.

There is a public jetty at the head of the bay, beyond which is Parsley Park. A light suspension bridge crosses the head of the bay.

VAUCLUSE BAY

This snug bay, at least to the writer, has the most charming suburban waterfront on the harbour. The waterside homes share an elegance and scale that seems just right. It is worth a visit but anchoring here is impracticable due to the density of the moorings. (*see* above)

NIELSEN PARK

Most of the promontory between Bottle and Glass Point and Steele Point is now part of the Sydney Harbour National Park. Access is via bush-walking tracks. Its rocky foreshore terminates in Shark Bay, tucked in behind Steele Point. A shark-proof swimming enclosure commands much of the 300 metre-long white sandy beach.

(Steele Point was previously known as Shark Point. The Aborigines called it Burroway, a considerably more romantic alternative.)

The term Shark Bay is rarely heard these days, the area more generally described as Nielsen Park, of which the bay is part. Nielsen Park, once owned by the pioneer Wentworth family, was named after the Minister of Lands who purchased it for public use soon after the turn of the century. The 1850s structures of Greycliffe House and the Gardner's Cottage remain a feature of Nielsen Park. Facilities include beach-showers, a kiosk and car park.

Vessels can stand close to the baths with about 3 metres depth off the pylons, though there a couple of rocks between the baths and the port beacon (off the northern end of the baths), so proceed with caution if you draft exceeds 2 metres.

Vessels should also be conscious of the large Prohibited Anchorage Area off Steele Point. You need to keep reasonably close-in in Shark Bay but the movement on all but the calmest days, particularly from passing wash, tends to discourage anchoring here.

TAYLORS BAY

On the opposite shores of the harbour is Taylors Bay, which has a sweeping and pleasant harbour outlook. Its walls are protected bush; it has generous depth; and it is rarely crowded. But you have to put up with some discomfort on all but the most favourable days because it is invariably troubled, not so much from wind waves as the joggle from the wash of passing traffic; and though it is protected from the brunt of the northeasterly sea breeze by the slopes of Chowder Head, random gusts can add to the frustration. It is worse in a southerly (and unthinkable when it is fresh). There are moorings around the head of the bay but there is ample room to anchor beyond them, though the preferred anchorage is tight in the lee of Chowder Head.

The steep slopes around the bay are part of the chain of reserves that form the Sydney Harbour National Park along the north shore. A delightful bush walk, which follows the escarpment, links the Bradleys Head with Middle Head.

The dress circle north shore suburb of Clifton Gardens is perched above the Chowder Head arm of the bay, the nearest street being Iluka Road. Access to the road is via steps in the northwest corner (look for dinghies) but it's a steep climb to the road and a long walk to the nearest shops at Mosman.

ROSE BAY

Rose Bay is the largest bay in the harbour, a broad horseshoe-shape stretching from Steele Point around to Woollahra Point. Its mouth — 1.6 kilometres wide — is distinctively marked by Shark Island, midway between the two points.

Vessels cruising Rose Bay should be conscious of the two large exclusion zones at the mouth: Naval Waters stretch from Steele Point to 400

metres north of Milk Beach and across to Shark Island; and between the southern end of Shark Island and Woollahra Point (see chart). Anchoring is forbidden in Naval Waters, though both these areas have too much movement to attract anyone but the desperate.

(The tiny cove of Hermit Bay, near Steele Point inside Rose Bay, is described under its own entry.)

Rose Bay's waters are flat, particularly inside Shark Island, though there's invariably some gentle movement in the bay — and it offers some protection from southerly gales at its head.

Much of the bay is navigable to within 50 or so metres of the shoreline, provided your draught does not exceed 2 metres.

The most notable exception is the southeast corner, which shoals to sand flats, much of which is exposed at low tide. Though moorings follow much of the shoreline at the head of the bay, there are few close to these shoals and you can profitably anchor around their perimeter where the water is deeper with good holding ground, a bonus should a southerly comes through.

Obviously you should proceed with due caution, but you can usually see the bottom. If the water is not clear, then you might employ two simple bearings to keep well clear of the shoal ground: draw an imaginary line from the lone steeple (to the left of the prominent Sacred Heart Convent on the eastern promontory) to the main public jetty at the head of the bay. If you keep to the Shark Island side of this imaginary line you should be well clear of the sandflats.

The eastern shores of the bay (north of the sandflats) offers opportunities for anchoring. Most of the waterfront is reserve, however, and access to services is that much more difficult. There is, however, an excellent walking track along the eastern shore, from below Sacred Heart Convent to Nielsen Park.

On the opposite side of the bay, moorings extend from Lyne Park around the southwest shores but it is easy enough to anchor beyond

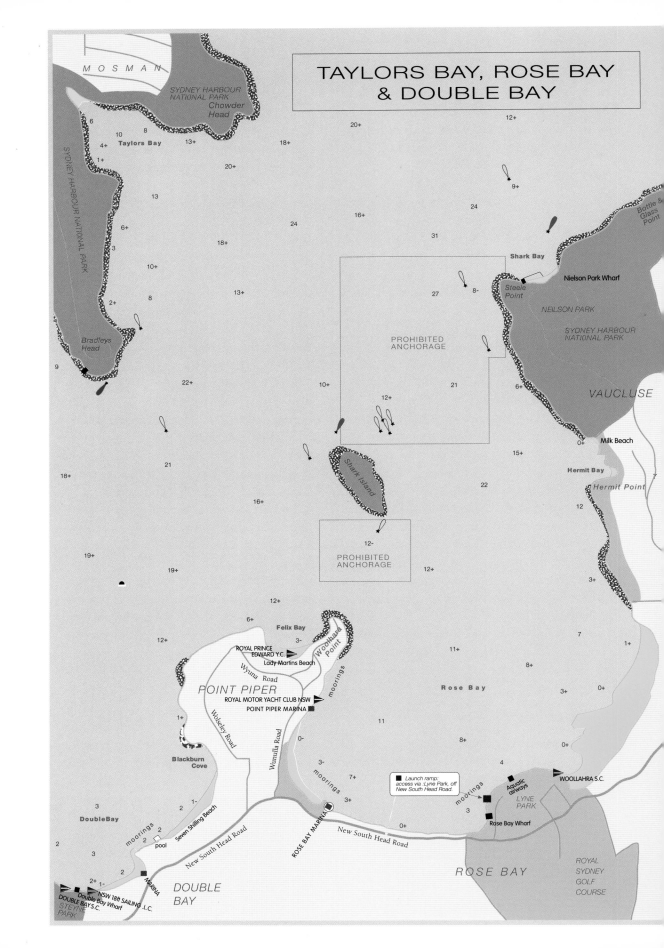

TAYLORS BAY, ROSE BAY & DOUBLE BAY

MOSMAN

SYDNEY HARBOUR
NATIONAL PARK
Chowder
Head

20+   12+

6
10   8
4+   Taylors Bay   13+   18+

1+   20+

SYDNEY HARBOUR
NATIONAL PARK

13

24

16+   24

9*

6+   18+

31

Bottle &
Glass
Point

Shark Bay

Nielson Park Wharf

8-   Steele
Point

NEILSON PARK

10+
8

13+

27

SYDNEY HARBOUR
NATIONAL PARK

2+

Bradleys
Head

21   22+

9

10+

12+

21

6+

VAUCLUSE

0+   Milk Beach

15-

Hermit Bay

Hermit Point

18+

16+   Shark Island

22

12

19+   19+

12-

PROHIBITED
ANCHORAGE

12+

3+

7

1+

12+

6+

Felix Bay

3-

12+

ROYAL PRINCE
EDWARD Y.C.

Lady Martins Beach

Wyuna   Road

POINT PIPER

ROYAL MOTOR YACHT CLUB NSW

POINT PIPER MARINA

Wolseley Road

1+

Blackburn
Cove

Wunulla Road

moorings

moorings

Woolhara
Point

11+

Rose Bay

8+

3+   0+

11

8+   0+

7+

Launch ramp:
access via :Lyne Park, off
New South Head Road.

moorings

Aquatic
airways   WOOLLAHRA S.C.

LYNE
PARK

0+

3

DoubleBay

2

3

moorings

2   2
pool

Seven Shilling Beach

New South Head Road

New South Head Road

0+

4

3

Rose Bay Wharf

ROSE BAY

ROYAL
SYDNEY
GOLF
COURSE

2+ 1-

Double Bay Wharf

DOUBLE BAY S.C.

STEYNE
PARK

NSW 18ft SAILING .L.C.

MARINA

ROSE BAY MARINA

DOUBLE
BAY

the moorings where the holding ground is good.

A particular advantage in cruising Rose Bay is the convenience of New South Head Road at its head, which leads to the city, and the substantial local shopping centre behind the southeast corner of the bay.

There are two well-established marinas in the bay. Rose Bay Marina stands in the southwest corner at the end of a sandy beach. It offers berths, moorings, two slips (for vessels of up to about 10 metres), a brokerage, repairs and petrol. It also has a restaurant on its premises, though there is no shortage of restaurants in Rose Bay, one of which is floating.

Point Piper Marina is on the western shore. It offers berths and a slipway for vessels up to 15 metres and both petrol and diesel fuels.

The adjacent Royal Motor Yacht Club is available for members only and their guests.

An entertaining element of Rose Bay is its flying boat service which takes-off and lands there on day trips to Pittwater, some 20 kilometres north as the crow flies — an exhilarating flight, especially if headed to one of Pittwater's delightful waterside restaurants. The small flying boat service is all that remains of Rose Bay's flying boat tradition that dates back to 1938. Qantas operated a flying boat service from the bay to the islands of Lord Howe, Norfolk and Hayman till the mid-1970s.

Lyne Park reserve, which has public toilets, lies on a blunt point that projects midway along the head of the bay, where activity is concentrated. This includes a Chinese floating restaurant, a public launching ramp (parking adjacent), public jetty and ferry wharf, Catalina Restaurant, the Flying Boat establishment, and the Woollahra Sailing Club, and a rowing club in the southeast corner.

There is a sea wall along much of the head of the bay, broken by landing steps about midway between the Chinese floating restaurant and the Rose Bay Marina.

Rose Bay was named by Governor Phillip for George Rose, the Secretary of the Treasury who was influential in financing the First Fleet.

HERMIT BAY

This tiny cove, a few hundred metres south of Steele Point on the eastern shores of Rose Bay features a small but sandy beach, divided by a rocky outcrop. Anchoring beyond moorings, with this delightful beach tucked in the southeast corner, has a great deal of charm, particularly with the shelter it offers from the usual northeast sea breezes. There's a small wharf (for small vessels only) alongside the tiny park on the point.

This stretch of Rose Bay offers a choice of three small beaches separated by two rocky knolls.

North of Hermit Bay is the diminutive cove of Milk Beach where, if you keep ten metres of so south of the portside navigation mark, you have 2-plus metres beneath you — and before you is the pleasing outlook of a small sandy beach behind which a path leads to the Nielsen Park Reserve. A little movement should be expected here.

South of Hermit is another (but unnamed) tiny sandy cove, with access to Queens Street. In fact, there are four beaches south of Hermit Bay which offer more depth. All of these are quite outside the prohibited area which is to the west.

FELIX BAY

Felix Bay occupies a small bight in the bluff head of the Point Piper headland, between Rose Bay and Double Bay.

Felix Bay is very exposed in most weather and vulnerable to passing commercial vessels. It's worth a pause because it is the home of the Royal Prince Edwards Yacht Club, which is available for members only and their guests. But quite apart from the movement, the bay is crowded with moorings.

MARINA WITH FUEL
MARINA
LAUNCHING RAMP
YACHT CLUB
RECREATIONAL AREA
STATE/NATIONAL PARKS
SAND, USUALLY MUDDY
ROCKS
MAJOR ROAD ACCESS
STARBOARD NAV LIGHT/BEACON
PORT NAV LIGHT/BEACON
WHITE/YELLOW NAV LIGHT/BEACON
MAXIMUM SPEED 4 KNOTS

SHARK ISLAND

Shark Island, which stands at the mouth of Rose Bay, was so named because its original natural shape looked (somewhat) like a shark. It is part of the chain of reserves around the harbour that comprise the Sydney Harbour National Park. Visitors to the island are required to make prior arrangement with the Parks and Wildlife Service. Prohibited naval waters lie immediately north and south of the island.

First gazetted as a recreational reserve in 1879, then used as a stock and dog quarantine station for a period, it was returned to the public domain under the Clark Island Trust. It is a delightful picnic ground with full amenities but sadly, you may not land there on a whim.

DOUBLE BAY

This is a broad, relatively sheltered bay, surrounded by high density suburbs and the fashionable shopping centre of Double Bay. The sandy strip of Seven Shillings Beach stretches from Blackburn Cove, tucked inside Point Piper, to the public baths near the head of the bay. Moorings are laid around the bay but there is room beyond them for anchoring, reasonable depth (4-plus metres at the outer moorings) and good holding ground.

The density of moorings at the head of the bay, however, make anchoring there impracticable — and the Double Bay public jetty at the head ensures periodic wash from ferries and water taxis in the quietest corners.

Also at the head of the bay is an agreeable sandy beach between the Double Bay Marina and the Double Bay Sailing Club. It offers a soft dinghy landing and ready access to shops and provisions of most kinds.

Steyne Park behind the beach has toilet facilities. A general store next Steyne Park is open seven days a week.

If you decide to anchor beyond the moorings, keep well clear of the navigation channel to the public jetty. Inside the moorings along Darling

NAVAL BUOYS

A dozen naval buoys like these are set around the main shipping channel. All fitted with lights. They are strictly reserved for shipping and you may not attache a mooring line to them in any circumstances.

Point, there is some 2 metres of water which shoals suddenly. Nevertheless, the writer has spent many happy hours anchored there, where the water is quietest.

East of the public jetty is the Double Bay Marina, which has berths, moorings, a slipway that can handle vessels up to 19 tonnes and diesel fuel.

DARLING POINT

The stretch of water off the long, bluff head of Darling Point is far too exposed for a comfortable anchorage. Furthermore it has a submarine cable between the point and Shark Island towards its eastern end and a broad mudflat shoal at its western end. In addition, the naval waters zone of the Man of War Anchorage extends from Garden Island, around Clark Island to within about 100 metresof Point Piper. The only practicable shore access in this stretch is via a small public reserve adjacent to McKell Park.

CLARK ISLAND

Prior arrangement must be made with the Parks and Wildlife Service before you may visit Clark Island. This island was named after Marine

The Cruising Yacht Club of Australia, Rushcutters Bay.

Lieutenant Ralph Cark who, in 1789, rowed to the island to establish a private garden, hoping it would prove remote enough to discourage the theft of his produce by convicts, Aborigines, or indeed, his fellow marines. It apparently discourage no-one and he soon abandoned the project.

Proclaimed a public reserve in 1879, it was subsequently doubled in size though reclamation to about a hectare. It was cultivated with largely exotic plants as a tourist attraction, though more recently a native garden has been developed. It is a delightful picnic spot.

RUSHCUTTERS BAY

The bustling head of Rushcutters Bay is the dominated by the Cruising Yacht Club of Australia complex, the high temple of ocean racing in Australia, the blue ribbon event of which is the Sydney-Hobart yacht race, one of the world's great ocean racing classics. The CYC, formed in World War II, initiated this now great

event in 1945, when a cruise to Hobart by a handful of yachts was transformed into a race, convincingly won by the distinguished British yachtsman, Captain John Illingworth.

This is a fascinating bay to visit, with its forest of masts and grand racing and cruising yachts, but it's no place to anchor. Quite apart from the density of the moorings, an area north of the CYC complex is a naval anchorage where private boats are prohibited.

If you wish to remain in the area, the CYC offers casual berths, which at the time of writing were at the rate of 70c per foot per day. This entitles you to the use of the club's deck facilities, showers, bars etc. One of the best times to go there is after Boxing Day, when the Hobart fleet has headed south.

The CYC has ice available for visitors but, like an increasing number of marinas, it no longer supplies fuel to visitors. It has a powerful slipway service that can accommodate vessels up to 80 tonnes.

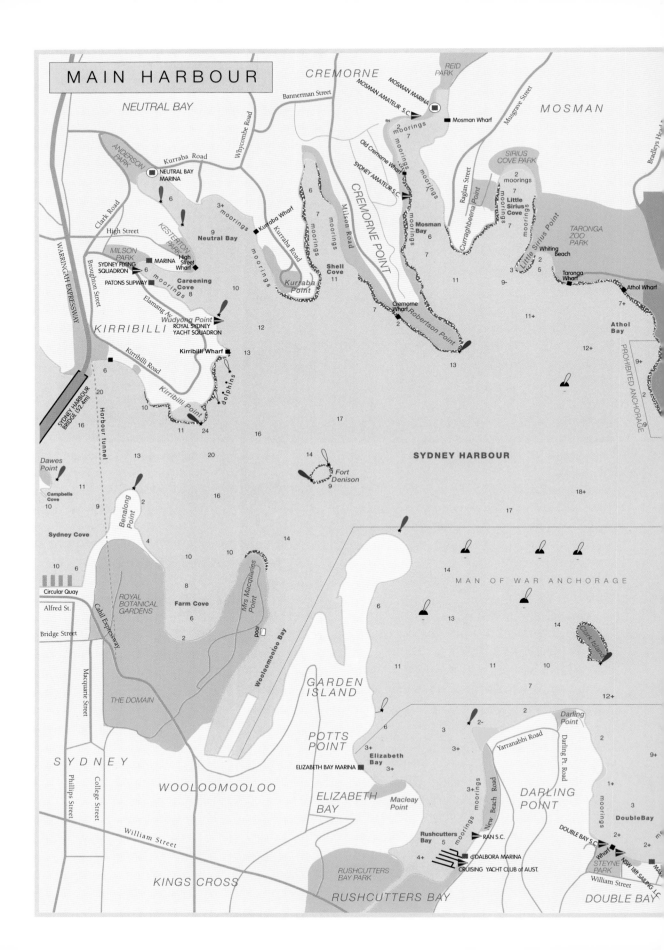

Immediately north of the CYC is the Rushcutters Bay Marina, operated by d'Albora Marinas. All services are available here including a fuel dock selling petrol and diesel. This is found at the inner end of the north arm on the northern side.

North of the moorings adjacent to Ruschcutters Bay Marina is a naval anchorage where private boats are prohibited.

The public park at the head of the bay — Rushcutters Bay Park — was reclaimed from marshlands. Early settlers used to cut reeds or rushes there for roof thatching, hence the name.

ELIZABETH BAY

Elizabeth Bay lies west of Rushcutters Bay on the Garden Island promontory, between Maclaey Point and Potts Point. It has good depth and holding ground but it is cluttered with moorings. It cannot be recommended for even a temporary stop, though you can drop a pick beyond the moorings, provided you do not interfere with the sometimes busy fairway to Rushcutters Bay.

Elizabeth Bay Park lies just inside the bay but a seawall makes access awkward.

Elizabeth Bay Marina has less than a dozen berths which are between piles and fixed pier. Ice is available as well as small boat haul-out, the cradle running up a railed ramp then onto a horizontal deck. There is a brokerage here but no fuel of any description. A general store nearby is well stocked.

Elizabeth Bay was named for the wife of the very able colonial Gover-

Fort Denison or "Pinchgut" — bold defender of the city behind it?

nor Lachlan Macquarie (1810-22), who was to be cruelly discredited by the infamous Bigge report.

The first landholder in the area was Alexander Macleay, Colonial Secretary of NSW from 1826 to 1837. His splendid mansion, Elizabeth Bay House, has been preserved and it is open to the public.

FORT DENISON

The martello-towered fort perched on the tiny island of Fort Denison off Woolloomooloo Bay looks almost surreal against the backdrop the aggressively modern skylines of Sydney and North Sydney, not to mention the avant-garde sails of the Sydney Opera House and the huge steel span of the Sydney Harbour Bridge. Perhaps it is too well-maintained for decay to give it a more convincingly historical appearance.

But historical it is, even if it never levelled its guns at an enemy. In fact, the only regular purpose its guns ever served was a daily shot to mark one o'clock from 1906 to World War II, after which the practice became too risky because of the ageing guns.

Once a barren rocky islet that eventually became known as Pinchgut, it was first used to maroon re-offending convicts on ships' biscuit and water as early as the first year of settlement. In 1796 a murderer was hung there in chains, his remains left hanging for some years as a deterrent to others.

(The emotive name Pinchgut, still used today by many, might seems obviously appropriate considering its historical use, but "Pinchgut" was once a maritime term used to describe a pinch in a navigable channel.)

In its original state, the island was a distinctive and apparently imposing rock outcrop that rose sheer from the harbour floor. That was before the colonial government, concerned by Sydney Harbour's vulnerability to attack in the early 19th century, decided to place a strategic gun battery there. (The Crimean War had raised a Russian spectre to add to the traditional foe, the French.) First the island was levelled to a flat top, and remained so for years before funds to build the fort became available. The fort was completed in 1857, with its martello tower built around the emplaced cannon, sealing them inside its walls. It was named after Governor Denison.

Other than a centre for gathering tidal information, the fort's main function today is a tourist attraction. Visits can be arranged through the Waterways authority.

GARDEN ISLAND

A harbour cruise around the naval establishment at Garden Island, particularly when warships are present, is invariably fascinating but anchoring or berthing there is strictly prohibited.

Once an island, it was first used for gardens at the time of First Settlement, primarily to reduce scurvy among the marines. Carved in a rock there are historic initials: F.M. 1788; I.B. 1788; and W.B. 1788. F.M. is believed to have been Frederick Meredith, a steward on the *Scarborough* in the First Fleet.

From 1883, Garden Island became a Royal Navy establishment, and by 1904, Australia's main naval base. It was subsequently transferred to the Royal Australian Navy, when the service was founded in 1911.

By 1940, a substantial dockyard had been proposed for Garden Island, involving the reclamation of some 14 hectares between the island and the mainland. More than a million tonnes of concrete were used in the project. The result was the Captain Cook Graving Dock, nearly 400 metres long and up to 100 metres wide. With up to 4000 working around the clock during World War II, it was one of Australia's truly great building projects.

In 1942, when three Japanese midget submarines entered the harbour, the SS *Kuttabul,* a former ferry, was employed as a depot ship at Garden Island. One of the submarines fired its torpedoes at a United States cruiser, the USS *Chicago*. The torpedoes missed the cruiser but one inadvertently sank the *Kuttabul* with a loss of 19 Australian sailors. That tragic "miss" was the only effective strike in the raid in which all three Japanese submarines were destroyed.

WOOLOOMOOLOO BAY

Narrow Wooloomooloo Bay is both deep and well-sheltered, an ideal cove for shipping. And there is splendid contrast in the lush green of Mrs Macquarie's Point on the western shores of bay and the busy maritime activity of the naval wharfs along Garden Island opposite.

At the head of the bay, which narrows to some 80 metres, is the historic Finger Wharf, the largest timber wharf on earth. It's future has been the subject of sometimes acrimonious debate for two decades, yet it remains uncertain, though apparently saved from demolition.

To the untutored eye, its timber piles seems as straight and symmetrical as they would have in its heyday, but its structure is apparently in bad shape. Overall, it looks sadly abandoned and dilapidated, with broken windows and faded signs. Whatever becomes of it, one hopes that it will retain some of its maritime identity as a once great working wharf.

The name Wooloomooloo, was taken from a local Aboriginal dialect, and is believed to be in some way associated with the kangaroo. In the 1840s, Wooloomooloo was an exclusive residential area and the city's fishmarkets were established at the head of the bay in the 1860s. With

Aerial shows Garden Island and Elizabeth Bay in the foreground, then Wooloomooloo Bay, Farm Cove, Sydney Cove and the Harbour Bridge. On the opposite shore is Kirribilli Point.

the increased maritime activity in the 1850s and the development of cheap dockside terraces the 'Loo became an increasingly disreputable tough neighbourhood and a breeding ground for "pushes" (street gangs) by the turn of the century, and particularly the 1930s.

Since then the area around the wharves — that had (by Australian standards) decayed to slums with a dwindling population — has been substantially redeveloped by the State Government. Compared with the infamous and exotic reputation of its past, the 'Loo today is distinctly orderly, even gentrified.

FARM COVE

You can take in the great landmarks of Sydney Harbour at a glance at Farm Cove, with the Opera House and the Harbour Bridge to the west and the towering central business district rising behind the lush precincts of the Botanical Gardens. To the north is the skyline of the twin city of North Sydney. You can even see the little sentinel of Fort Denison.

Unfortunately, you may not anchor overnight here, nor may you land in the precincts of the botanical Gardens after closing, for obvious reasons. But it a charming spot to take visitors in daylight hours.

Depths are 2 metres to 7 or more and the holding ground is good. The waters are well-sheltered, though passing traffic causes occasional wash. Man of War wharf, in the lee of the Opera House, is the only commercial traffic destination in the precincts of the cove, and it is tucked into Bennelong Point, well away from the mouth of the cove. You may drop the pick where you choose in Farm Cove: it is one of precious few harbour coves with no moorings.

The cove is formed in a sweeping symmetrical curve, bordered by an immaculate seawall. Mrs Macquaries Point reserve is an excellent place to go shore, with access to the city.

A feature at the point is Mrs Macquarie's Chair, which was carved out of stone around 1816 for Governor Macquarie's lady, so that she might more comfortably enjoy the view.

Farm Cove takes its name from its first purpose at the time of First Settlement. The little colony's first livestock grazed there. The present reserves around the bays two headlands are divided between: The Domain, a 70 hectare of green belt that stretches from Mrs Macquarie's Point inland along the eastern side of the city centre; and the Botanical Gardens, which occupy much of Bennelong Point to the Opera House, covering some 26 hectares. The Botanical Gardens was started in 1816. Government House and the old Conservatorium of Music adjoin the gardens.

Farm Cove, calm waters, and cultivated to the water's edge.

BENNELONG POINT

Bennelong Point is the headland that divides Farm Cove from Sydney Cove. Vessels must stand off from the Opera House at its tip by at least 120 metres. It is an extremely busy stretch of water and anchorage in its vicinity is strictly forbidden.

Once a tiny island, Bennelong Point was joined to the mainland in 1817. It takes its name from the character Bennelong, an Aboriginal befriended by Governor Phillip and for whom he built a brick hut there.

Later a small fort was built there. It was eventually replaced by a tram depot, which was demolished to make way for the Sydney Opera House.

The Sydney Opera House straddles Bennelong Point, with the Royal Botanical Gardens to the east, Sydney's central business districts behind it, and Circular Quay to the west. The base of the Opera House is a monolithic concrete podium covering nearly two hectares. It houses scores of rooms for performers and services, plus the drama theatre, recording hall, music room and cinema. The podium is clad with distinctive pink NSW granite. Utzon had wanted this cladding to end above the water-line to create an impression that the Opera House was floating above the water.

Three groups of soaring shells rise from the podium, the highest reaching the equivalent of 20 storeys. The largest group of shells cover the concert hall; the smaller group covers the Opera theatre. Much smaller shells, hidden from the harbour, house the Bennelong Restaurant.

The Sydney Opera House is inspiring from literally any viewing angle. Universally recognised as one of the truly great buildings of the world, it is a source of great pride to Australians. Sydneysiders feel a more personal, intimate affection.

The Opera House is not only a temple for the city's artistic aspirations, it has also become a natural centre for a remarkably wide range of entertainment that reaches the wider community. Controversial from it outset, Sydney Opera House was designed, though sadly not completed, by Danish architect, Joern Utzon. The final stages were completed by a team of local architects. When costs escalated tenfold to more than $100 million, a typically Australian solution was found — the Opera House Lotteries. The Opera House was opened by Queen Elizabeth II in 1973.

SYDNEY COVE

Its astonishing how many Sydneysiders have

difficulty placing Sydney Cove, though they have no problem directing you to "Circular Quay", the main harbour ferry terminal which dominates its head.

Though Sydney Cove was the place of birth for Sydney and the nation, the name seems increasingly confined to its historical context in popular use, though it remains, of course, on maps and nautical charts.

This seems a pity, considering its monumental significance. Perhaps Sydneysiders take it for granted.

An evocative if somewhat obscure comparison might be drawn between the glamour and clamour of Sydney Cove and the simple memorial to Formby Sutherland at the water's edge in Botany Bay.

Sutherland was the first European to be buried on the east coast of Australia. A humble seaman with Cook, he died of tubercolosis. His shipmates ferried his body ashore at Botany Bay and buried him just beyond the high-water mark — a miserable end in a lonely grave in an unknown land, far from home. Then his ship sailed away, never to return.

By comparison, Sydney Cove carried the first bright hopes with the birth of settlement and little more than 200 years later has become a dazzling reflection of the achievement and confidence of a nation that had tranformed those alien shores. In the process it gave the abandoned Formby Sutherland a place in history — a lasting memorial that he could never have dreamed of in the normal course of his humble life.

The Opera House gracing Bennelong Point, is not only Australia's noblest cultural asset, it is universally acknowledged; the Harbour Bridge that meets Dawes Point was one the great engineering feats of its time; the bold glass and concrete towers of the city skyline reflect contemporary substance and radiate confidence; and The Rocks, though gentrified, are a reminder of a past measured in generations rather than centuries. Should Canberra last 1000 years and build countless more monumental edifices, it could not compare. Because Sydney Cove has much more than splendid surrounds. It is where white settlement began.

Sydney Cove was chosen in 1788 by the colony's first Governor, Captain Arthur Phillip, because it offered shelter for his ships, deep water close-in and, crucially, a small freshwater creek that emptied into its northeast corner, and surrounding forests for timber.

Phillip discovered the cove on January 23, sailed the *HMS* Supply around from Botany Bay on January 25 and had the rest of the fleet anchored there by January 26. With more than 200 years of hindsight, Phillip's choice of Sydney Cove remains the perfect one.

Circular Quay took its name from earlier configuration of the cove; an 1874 illustration shows the seawall around its head following an almost perfectly circular sweep. Today, the blunt head of the cove is dominated by the floating fingers of five ever-busy ferry wharves. Sydney Harbour's ferries shift 3 million passengers a year.

On the western shores of the cove, the Overseas Passenger Terminal presents visitors with a dockside panorama on arrival that few ports in the world could challenge. (Some 25 passenger vessels make around 75 calls to Sydney Harbour each year.)

The view is all you are entitled to because unauthorised vessels are strictly forbidden from entering Sydney Cove's busy precincts for obviously sound reasons. When passing the entrance to the bay, stand off at least 120 metres from the beacons on both headlands.

The stretch of water from Kirribilli Point, under the Harbour Bridge, to about midway past Lavender Bay, can be the most confused in the harbour. (The entrance, of course, can be much rougher in heavy weather but the swells tend to come from one direction.) The cause of the confusion around the bridge is a combination of the narrowing of the waterway at this point and the wash churned-up by the ferries and other traffic. This is no place to put the coffee on or to take your eyes off the children. If you have visitors aboard, especially the frail or the timid, advise them to sit somewhere secure. We are not talking about dangerous waters but movement can be surprisingly violent and irregular, quite sufficient to gybe the boom suddenly enough on a light day to alarm your guests or slosh a bucketful into the cockpit. On the other hand, this confusion lasts only a short stretch and it provides a dramatic view of Sydney for visitors. Children of all ages are awed by the bridge passing more than 50 metres above.

Anchorage in this area is largely banned. And it would be unthinkable even if it were not.

HARBOUR TUNNEL

The Sydney Harbour 4-lane traffic tunnel runs beneath the harbour on the eastern side of the bridge. It enters the harbour at Milsons Point and exits on the western side of Sydney Cove, emerging alongside the Domain. It was completed in 1992.

Though a complex feat of engineering, the concept for construction was ingeniously simple. First, a channel was dredged. Then a series of gigantic prefrabricated concrete tubes, their ends sealed, were towed to the site. These were then flooded, lowered into the trench, joined, sealed and the water pumped out — and so on.

The tunnel sits below the level of the harbour floor, which itself is well over 12 metres deep in this section.

SYDNEY HARBOUR BRIDGE

The gigantic steel arch of Sydney Harbour Bridge, the most obvious landmark in the harbour, divides this great waterway roughly in half. From the bridge to North harbour is the Lower Harbour; and from the bridge to the narrows of the Parramatta River is the Upper Harbour, the two sections are of comparable length if not volume. It is the simplest division of the harbour and the one we chose for this book (compared with the more refined distinctions between, Port Jackson, Sydney Harbour, main harbour etc).

The bridge, completed in 1932, links the twin cities of Sydney and North Sydney, spanning Dawes and Milsons points. It was the biggest single span bridge in the world then, and a rousing morale boost for the country during the Depression (1929-35), a grim period in Australia's history that wreaked massive unemployment, financial ruin and economic collapse on a generation of Australians. The bridge not only provided work for thousands, it helped to restore the nation's battered self-confidence.

Sydney Harbour Bridge has a headway of 52 metres, its deck, which carries eight road lanes and two rail tracks, is more than 500 metres long and its top span soars to 134 metres above sea level — all of which is held together by 6 million huge steel rivets.

Public access to the pylon lookout on Dawes Point is via Cumberland Street.

BRADLEYS HEAD

The long narrow promontory of Bradleys Head is the most prominent and significant landform on the north shore. It marks the point at which the harbour tends from a southerly direction to a generally westerly aspect that carries all the way to the Parramatta River.

This is arguably the most dangerous corner on the harbour, though it is marked by a lighthouse at its tip, occulting green (three seconds).

There is good depth to within ten metres of the lighthouse but vessels should be very conscious of the rocky ledge north-to-northeast of the light. It altered countless keels before the cardinal mark was finally set there. If it claims fewer keels these days, fewer is the operative word.

Cruising vessels should keep well clear of the point when rounding because of its blind side. This is one of those exceptional situations in which hugging the starboard side to keep clear of approaching traffic is a poor option. (The same applies to Cremorne Point and Kirribilli Point). Prudence dictates you keep well clear of the point

The Sydney Harbour Bridge, joining North Sydney to the city. Kirribilli Point is shown on the right.

to open up a wider view around the blind side to track approaching traffic as early as practicable (and for approaching vessels to spot you!)

A considerable amount of traffic rounds the point, including the swift jetcat ferries. It is certainly no place for cruising vessels on race days during summer, particularly in a northeaster, when racing fleets converge on the point and tack within metres of the lighthouse as they work up the harbour. This can not only present a wall of boats at the point — all sailing under yacht racing rules and often aggressively — but boats moving at a confusing variety of speeds.

The most awe-inspiring of these are the 18-footers, which seem to approach the point with the caution of kamikaze pilots. They are (mostly) skilled athletes who sail with spectacular daring and admirable elan, but judging your angle of intersection with an 18-footer in a spanking breeze (or worse, a gusting breeze) is one of harbour sailing's grand illusions. It's worth remembering that at the point of tacking they come almost to a standstill, with limited manoeuvrability till they regain sufficient way.

Close calls with the "aydeens" can trigger ship-to-ship conversation more robust than that condoned in the raw bear pit of State Parliament. Apologies from miscreants are anecdotal. (It must have happened, but no-one has actually heard an 18-footer skipper admit fault.) But then their sailing adds a spectacular dimension to Sydney Harbour, and their gung-ho history has a special place in the local culture.

Behind the lighthouse at Bradleys Head stands the steel tripod mast of HMAS *Sydney*, which sank the feared German raider, the *Emden*, in Indian

Ocean in 1914.

Though the author has expressed concern at the diminishment of maritime industry and the naval presence in Sydney Harbour, few would regret the recent removal of the large naval jetties in Athol Bay, just off the western aspect of Bradleys Head, least of all racing yachtsmen. It was used largely to moor the navy's mothball fleet, including those vessels destined for scrapping — and most looked like they were overdue by a generation or more.

The removal of the ships and the jetty, however, does not appear to have opened this area up for anchorage. The Waterways chart of July, 1997, still marks the zone to the west of Bradleys Head as naval waters and thus a prohibited anchorage.

The land covering Bradleys Head is mostly bushland, with a small park at its tip that is a popular picnic ground with splendid all-round harbour views. There are public toilets in the park and historcal gun emplacements.

Bradleys Head can be visited by car or ferry, though an entry fee is levied on vehicles on weekends. Bushwalking tracks link with Little Sirius Cove to the west (which includes a stretch of road past the zoo wharf) and northward to Middle Head, which is all bushland.

Bradleys Head, was named for Lieutenant William Bradley RN, of the HMS *Sirius*, flagship of the First Fleet. Bradley, with Captain John Hunter, began sounding and charting the harbour within days of First Settlement.

The gun pit near the tip of the head was built by the colonial administration in 1841, a powder magazine and stone gallery added 30 years later. These fortifications were gazetted part of the National Estate in 1978.

ATHOL BAY

The recent removal of the longstanding navy jetty for its mothball fleet from Athol Bay has not only splendidly opened up the bay but increased opportunities for the cruising boating man.

The naval waters off the western shores of Bradleys Head that used to surround the jetties there, remain naval waters, according to the latest Waterways Chart (July, 1997). The naval mooring buoy near the middle of the bay — Athol No 4 — also remains.

But beyond the naval zone, tucked snug into the northeast corner of the bay, and too tiny even to call a cove, is an unnamed but charming sandy beach that makes a delightful anchorage. It is well sheltered, though some movement must be expected, particularly from the zoo ferries. But it offers access to the Bradleys Head reserve behind it and there is plenty of depth off the shore, shoaling to about 2 metres some 30 metres off the beach.

Taronga Zoo dominates the northern slopes at the head of Athol Bay, which keeps the zoo ferry wharf at the western end of the bay busy with a regular stream of tourists.

In fact, Taronga, with its matchless elevated outlook across the harbour to the city, has remained popular since it was open in 1916. More than 400,000 people visited it in its first year. The zoo has a history of innovative display, eschewing bars where practicable in favour of moats and similarly discrete fencing, along with preserving much of the native flora on the site.

The zoo's current policy is to concentrate on the quality of its exhibits rather than quantity, and to develop its educational potential. Nearly 100,000 schoolchildren visit the zoo each year. The zoo also uses its expertise to help injured native animals so that they may be returned to the wild. With is sister zoo — the Western Plains Zoo at Dubbo — it has treated more than 1000 such animals.

Australia's first conservation research centre, which cooperates with other wildlife and scientific institutions, was established at the zoo in 1989.

WHITING BEACH

If you don't mind a little bobbing about, this

charming little cove is nearly perfect. The bay offers about 2-plus metres depth about a third of the way in (from its two points) and a lovely sandy beach. Above the beach — steps in the northwest corner — is a path which is part of the Sydney Harbour National Park walk. It is only some 150 metres along the path to the zoo bus terminal and ferry wharf. In the opposite direction, it's about a kilometre walk along Little Sirius Point to the head of Little Sirius Cove and the streets of Mosman.

A salutary word of caution, which probably applies anywhere is the harbour: chain your dinghy if you have to leave it on the beach for any period. (The author had his stolen there while ashore visiting Mosman.)

Another tip for harbour beaches, particularly the less popular beaches, and particularly for children: wear shoes of some sort! Despite the wonderful harbour cleanups inspired by the heroic Ian Kiernan, drug users are shamefully careless with the disposal of used needles. They are apparently drawn to the beaches at night, and not only during the summer months. Evidence of this was not "exposed" in a tabloid newspaper, but observed at a few relatively remote harbour beaches during the research for this book — abandoned beach camp fires with discarded needles laying nearby. Storm water drains also wash all manner of suspicious looking detritus down to some beaches and it pays to keep well away from these outlets.

At the risk of straying beyond the scope of this book, the rubbish with which we continue to litter and pollute the priceless gift of Sydney Harbour remains depressing, even though is appears to be diminishing. Stormwater drains and industrial waste

aside, the cause more often than not seems to be laziness or ignorance, though sometimes it is wilful contempt.

The complex sociological issues of drug use is certainly beyond the realm of this text, but users who carelessly discard their needles on invitingly sandy beaches, where tiny feet may innocently scamper, seems to me beyond contempt. They are assuredly aware of risks associated with discarded needles, risks much more terrible than a sudden sharp jab, no matter how painful. Such callous indifference is surely evil.

LITTLE SIRIUS COVE

This pleasant little cove is better enjoyed from the shore than afloat because it is packed with moorings. In the unlikely event you can squeeze in somewhere, its advantages are the popular Little Sirius Cove Park behind a sandy beach at its head, and access to water taps and public toilets in the park. The many dinghies chained in the northeast corner of the cove indicate the best landing spot. There are, however, no shops in the vicinity.

MOSMAN BAY

Though regarded by many as the most charming bay on Sydney Harbour, public access is so limited here that it is near impossible to get

Pretty Little Sirius Cove.

Cremorne Point viewed from Mosman Bay. Fort Denison is in the middle distance.

ashore. The eastern banks of the bay, apart from the Musgrave Street ferry wharf near Curraghbeena Point, is lined with the homes of the fortunate. There is a small strip of public reserve above the opposing (Cremorne Point) shores, but there are discouraging rocks around the water's edge and steep wooded slopes beyond. Moorings are dense along both shores, particularly at the head of the bay where they are crammed in fore-and-aft.

There is, however, a small pond, surrounded by a seawall at the extreme head of the bay, past the marina, where at least a temporary anchorage can be made with a stern line to the seawall. There's only about 2 metres-plus in the pond.

Mosman Bay is busy and the navigation channel must be respected. Three ferry wharfs service this narrow bay till late at night: Musgrave Street on the eastern point; Old Cremorne about two thirds into the bay on the Cremorne Point shoreline; and the Mosman ferry wharf at the head. Beyond the wharf is the Mosman Bay Marina, the Mosman Rowing Club, a popular casual dining spot. The Mosman Amateur Sailing Club is to the west of the "Rowers".

The Mosman Bay Marina has both pens and moorings and a slipway with a capacity for boats up to 45 feet. It supplies both ice and diesel fuel (no petrol) to the public.

The small but charming Sydney Amateur Sailing Club is situated midway along the Cremorne Point banks. Its facilities are available to members and their guests but the small slipway and repair service is available to the public. Mosman Bay was originally named Great Sirius Cove because HMS *Sirius* was careened there in 1789. (It was commonplace for large ships of that time to beach themselves so that the bottom could be cleaned or repaired when exposed at low tide.)

Mosman Bay is named after Archibald Mosman, who established a whaling station there in 1830. Though half the income of New South Wales in the mid-1830s was derived from whale oil and bone, the industry, including the Mosman Bay station, collapsed in the 1840s. It was to become one of the most sought after residential addresses on the north shore. A visit by boat explains why.

Opposite: Passengers ships enter the very heart of the city at Sydney Cove — an imposing front door for the nation.

SHELL COVE

This is a long, narrow cove with mud flats at its head. There is no commercial traffic and its usually quite calm but it is crowded with moorings. Shore access is not easy because it is surrounded by steep banks with wall-to-wall houses and home units along the western shore and the Cremorne reserve to the east. It's a bit of a scramble up the eastern shore, though there are steps to the reserve just inside the bay — or a long row to Cremorne ferry wharf, the bonus of which is a handy shop and a regular bus service, linked with the ferry. There is about 8 metres depth in the middle of the bay, 5 metres at the limit of moorings at the head of the bay and 6-plus along the western shore. There's a tiny jetty on the western shore with access to the main road but you may not anchor near it.

NEUTRAL BAY

This is really a broad, double-bay, the western section forming Neutral Bay proper and the eastern, Careening Cove. It is of interest because of the activity there rather than as a cruising destination. This bay that can fairly bustle, with its three ferry wharves, the submarine docks of HMAS *Platypus* and the Neutral Bay Marina at its head, not to mention moorings strung around the navigation channels for both Neutral Bay and Careening Cove. (The future of HMAS *Platypus* remains uncertain at the time of writing.)

Neutral Bay stretches north from Kurraba Point, which has a pleasant park beneath the point's sandstone crop. The navigation channel to Kurraba Wharf, lined with moorings, must be kept clear.

Further round the bay is the Neutral Bay Wharf. An inner cove — part of the bay — starts at the Neutral Bay wharf, inside of which is a private jetty, followed by the Customs establishment, slipways and the Captain Cook Ferry terminal at its head. The Neutral Bay Marina offers full marine services and a large slipway.

Home units dominate the head, with North Sydney business district skyline behind.

HMAS *Platypus* wharf is situated along the western shore and the North Sydney (High Street) Ferry Wharf at the tip of Kesterton Park on the western point.

Neutral Bay is strictly a business zone. It is not for cruising.

CAREENING COVE

Careening Cove, which extends along the shores of Kirribilli, opens on to Neutral Bay. As the present name suggests, the bay was once used for careening ships, the sandy beach where the vessels were beached long since reclaimed to form Milson Park. The bay was also, for a time, known as Slaughterhouse Bay when a slaughteryard was operated there.

The ramp at the foot of Milson Park is for the exclusive use of the historic 18 foot skiff club, the Sydney Flying Squadron, formed in 1890, which is tucked into the western corner of bay.

The Ensemble Theatre stands alongside, and beyond that Patons Slipway, which can accommodate vessels of up to 110 tonnes. It has 4 cradles and offers a full range of services including shipwrights, engineering, painting, welding, and electrical work. There is also a brokerage.

A string of offices along the northeastern shores at the head of the bay accommodates a number of marine specialists, such as folding propellers and sails, as well as non marine occupants, attracted by the view. Beyond the building is a spray painter's slipway.

The southern Kirribilli shores of Careening Cove are lined with units and private homes. Dominating the southern headland at Wudyoung Point is the splendid Royal Sydney Yacht Squadron, which operates one of few travel lifts on the harbour (as opposed to slipways). Squadron facilities are available to members and their guests.

Beyond the Royal Sydney Yacht Squadron is the Kirribilli ferry wharf.

UPPER HARBOUR

FUEL : LAVENDER BAY, BERRYS BAY, BALMAIN, BIRKENHEAD POINT
PUBLIC LAUNCHING RAMPS : MANNS POINT, CLARKES POINT

FROM LAVENDER BAY TO CLARKES POINT ON THE NORTHERN SHORE

LAVENDER BAY

The first bay west of the Sydney Harbour Bridge along the northern shore, is Lavender Bay, flanked by Milsons Point and McMahons Point. It is far too cluttered with moorings to consider as an anchorage. Submarine cables that cross the mouth prohibit anchoring there and the moorings are too dense to contemplate a spot amongst them. Added to this is the movement on the bay, largely generated by the shop around thebridge and ferry traffic.

The shores of Lavender Bay are completely developed. The North Sydney Olympic pool is situated near the tip of Milsons Point, which forms the eastern shore. Beyond that is Luna Park, behind the Milsons Point ferry wharf, and beyond Luna Park is the railway marshalling yards — all set against a backdrop of the north Sydney business district.

At the head of the bay is the Lavender Bay Wharf, used by commercial and charter vessels and in the northwestern corner stands the Sunsail offices and a very small public ramp, where you will have to cross a small sandy beach at low tide. The western shores are packed tight with apartment buildings and private homes. The half a dozen jetties there are all private.

Right on the point, behind the MacMahons Point ferry wharf, stands the seafood restaurant, Sails.

Beyond McMahons Point, there is a small bight in the headland that terminates at Blues Point. It accommodates a small slipway available to private vessels. If you must anchor in this bay and can tolerate the movement, then this is the best spot. You can land a dinghy at the steps in the middle of the sea wall. A small strip of sand is exposed at low tide. Behind the sea wall is a narrow reserve, behind which is Henry Lawson Avenue (it intersects Blues Point Road, which will lead to shops if you need supplies).

The most dominant feature of the bay is, of course, Luna Park. This a fun park has been part of the Sydney cultural landscape since its opening in 1935. It's familiar grinning face has had precious little to smile about recently.

This park ran virtually interrupted — even during the blackouts in World War II — till 1979, when an horrific fire on the "Ghost Train" claimed an adult and six children. The park was subsequently closed, remodelled, and reopened — only to be closed again as a result of a dispute with some residents who complained of the noise level. Its future, clouded by complex litigation, remains uncertain. Fun, it seems, has been banned there, probably for good.

The adjacent North Sydney Olympic Pool has a happier story. It not only boasts more than 80 world records, set by such great Australian swimmers as

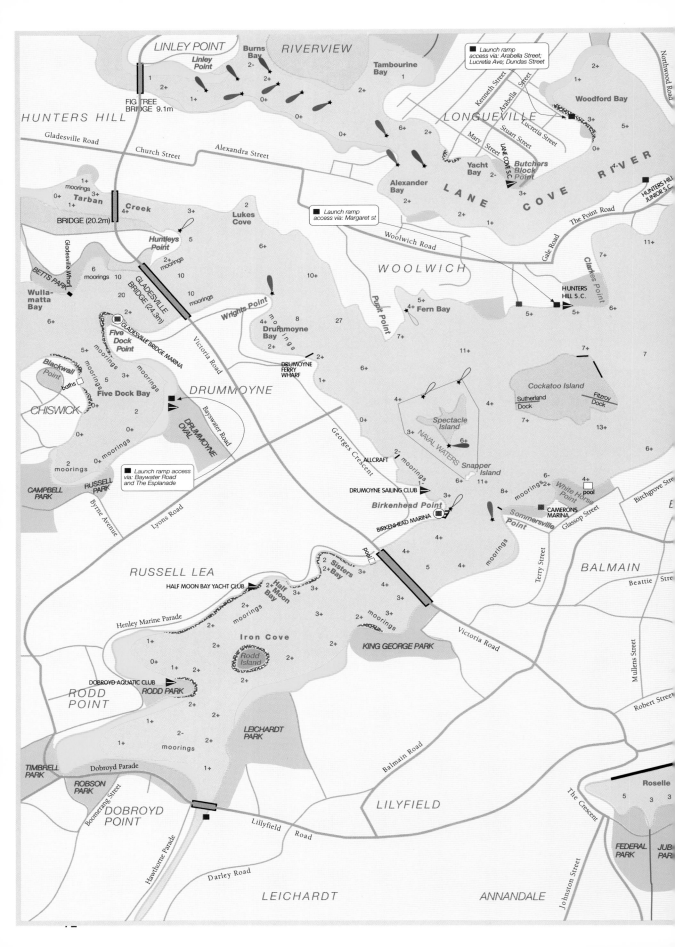

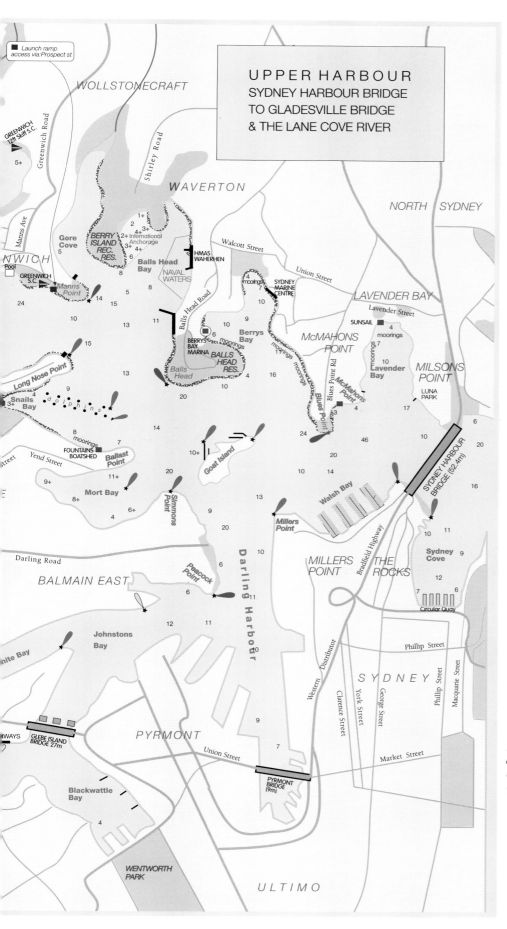

Launch ramp
access via: Prospect st

UPPER HARBOUR
SYDNEY HARBOUR BRIDGE
TO GLADESVILLE BRIDGE
& THE LANE COVE RIVER

WOLLSTONECRAFT

GREENWICH
12ft Skiff S.C.

5+

Greenwich Road

Manns Ave

Shirley Road

WAVERTON

NORTH SYDNEY

Gore
Cove
5

BERRY
ISLAND
REC.
RES.

1+
2
3+
2+ International
3+ Anchorage
4+
6

Walcott Street

Union Street

NWICH

Pool

GREENWICH
S.C.

Manns
Point

14

15

24

10

15

13

11

Balls Head Road

Balls Head
Bay

HMAS
WAHERHEN

NAVAL
WATERS

moorings
7

SYDNEY
MARINE
CENTRE

10

LAVENDER BAY

Lavender Street

SUNSAIL

McMAHONS
POINT

4
moorings

LAVENDER
BAY

MILSONS
POINT

Long Nose Point

dolphins

Snails
Bay
3+

4

8
moorings
7

FOUNTAINS
BOATSHED

Ballast
Point

Yend Street

9+

Mort Bay
8+

11+

6+

4

Simmons
Point

BERRYS
BAY MARINA

6

moorings

BALLS
HEAD
RES.

Balls
Head

13

20

14

10+

Goat Island

20

10

13

20

Berrys
Bay

16

Blues Point Rd

Blues Point

24

McMahons
Point

4

LUNA
PARK

17

46

20

14

SYDNEY HARBOUR
BRIDGE (52.4m)

6

20

10

16

10

11

Walsh Bay

Millers
Point

MILLERS
POINT

THE
ROCKS

Bradfield Highway

Sydney
Cove
12

9

Circular Quay
7   6

Darling Road

BALMAIN EAST

Peacock
Point

6

11

12

11

Johnstons
Bay

nite Bay

Darling Harbour

Western Distributor

Phillip Street

SYDNEY

Phillip Street

Macquarie Street

Clarence Street

York Street

George Street

9

WAYS

GLEBE ISLAND
BRIDGE 27m

PYRMONT

Union Street

7

PYRMONT
BRIDGE
(9m)

Market Street

Blackwattle
Bay

4

WENTWORTH
PARK

ULTIMO

MARINA WITH FUEL
MARINA
LAUNCHING RAMP
YACHT CLUB
RECREATIONAL AREAS
STATE/NATIONAL PARKS
SAND, USUALLY MUDDY
ROCKS
MAJOR ACCESS
STARBOARD NAV LIGHT/BEACON
PORT NAV LIGHT/BEACON
WHITE/YELLOW NAV LIGHT/BEACON
4k   MAXIMUM SPEED 4 KNOTS

73

Dawn Fraser, the Konrads and Shane Gould, but it remains a popular and significant venue for a sport in which Australians now expect to excel.

Lavender Bay is named for George Lavender, a ferryman from the 1830s in the tradition of Billy Blue. Indeed, he married Billy's daughter Suzannah. Lavender shot himself in 1851.

BLUES POINT

Takes its name from Billy Blue, a black boatman, who was granted 32 hectares at the point in 1817. He rowed his produce to Millers Point and eventually incorporated a ferry service in his trips.

BERRYS BAY

Following the northern shore, the second bay upstream from the harbour bridge is Berrys Bay. Anchoring is possible in this bay but it is difficult to keep out of harms way. Nevertheless it has a number of interesting features, not all of which are edifying.

Blues Point, at the entrance to the bay, is dominated by Blues Point Towers, a tall, narrow, featureless column of units in pale brick, widely regarded as the ugliest and most inappropriate building on the harbour.

Just inside the point is the narrow but very pleasant Sawmillers Reserve. A seawall extends along its length, a feature of which is the hulk of an old barge nestling against it. A small public jetty extends from the reserve and there are steps in the seawall if you wish to land a dinghy. There is uncomfortable movement from passing traffic near the mouth of the bay and it cannot be generally recommended, though it is deep water with good holding ground.

Tucked into the western bight of the bay (inside Balls Head) is Berrys Bay Marina. Its slipway is used more by commercial than private boats. Owners may not work on their own boats there.

Further into the bay, along the western shoreline, stands the BP Flammable Liquids Berth, from which vessels are required to keep clear.

Opposite, on the western side of the bay, is the huge marine complex of the Sydney Marine Centre, where all manner of marine services are available with slipways capable of hauling out vessels of 100 tonnes. It is also a terminal commercial ferries and cruise boats.

The Waverton Park reserve lies at the head of the bay and the Balls Head, which marks the western headland, is a large and popular picnic area. It has historical interest, too, because it is one of few sites of Aboriginal rock engravings and hand stencils that survives in the metropolitan Sydney.

Berrys Bay was named for Alexander Berry (1781-1873), a one-time surgeon and then ship owner. He formed a business partnership with Edward Wollstonecraft, after whom a nearby suburb is named.

The head, now known as the Berrys Island reserve, was once a tidal island that was joined to the point in the 1960s.

BALLS HEAD BAY

This relatively broad bay forms a double bay near its head — the narrowing eastern cove is called Wollstonecraft Bay and the unnamed western cove is the harbour's International Small Craft Anchorage.

Balls Head forms the eastern headland at the entrance to the bay, which is dominated by the massive stone ramparts and the heavy jetty of the long defunct coal loading facility. The coal loading jetty was never a pretty sight but its timbers are now so obviously rotten that only its steel skeleton appears to be keeping it upright. It seems to serve no purpose but if its unprepossessing looks are not a deterrent, it is well positioned in good depth and muddy ground for good holding. It can be handy to anchor in its lee for a short stop.

Further inside the bay, along the eastern shoreline, is HMAS *Waterhen*, a large naval establishment. Both the coal loader and HMAS *Waterhen* are out of bounds to visitors and in the latter's case the waters off HMAS *Waterhen* are designated naval waters, which means you may pass through them but you may not anchor.

The western headland is part of the Berry Island Recreational Reserve, which extends around the shores of the international anchorage and on to Wollstonecraft Bay. Adjacent to the reserve at the head of the bay is the old gasworks site, which is currently being redeveloped, though it is to be hoped that some of the old building and its landmark chimney might be preserved.

As mentioned, the Berry Island reserve extends around the shores of the well-protected international anchorage bay. There it offers an easy landing for dinghies and shore access to Balls Head Road, which leads to Wollstonecraft station — though a longish walk. This bay is out of bounds to all by international cruisers and the writer could not test this anchorage, but Alan Lucas said in his landmark 1991 book that there can be occasional difficulties with old cables and suchlike on the bottom.

Balls Head Bay is named after Lieutenant Henry Lidgbird Ball R.N., who commanded HMS *Supply* of the First Fleet. He played a significant role in the exploration and charting of the harbour and later discovered Lord Howe Island.

GORE COVE

This narrow inlet between Berry Island and Mann Point can be easily missed or ignored at first glance. This is a pity because despite the string of singularly unprepossessing oil tanks along the western point it is a sweet little cove, well out of harm's way.

The Berry Island reserve stretches along its eastern shore and the head of the bay is densely wooded with few houses visible.

Anchoring is a problem: the navigation channel needs to be kept open and many of the moorings are ranged fore-and-aft to accommodate it. But it may be possible to squeeze into a couple of spots if you take a little time, considerable care and some discretion.

This cove is deep in most parts but if you enter at high tide don't be misled — the water shoals quite suddenly to muddy shallows at the head, most of which is exposed at low tide. Proceed beyond the oil terminal's seawall (or inside the innermost moorings) at your peril. There's about 2 metres along that line but the ground shoals sharply beyond it.

You can land a dinghy at the Berry Island reserve and follow Shirley Street all the way to Crows Nest; or enjoy the delightful nature walk to Wollstonecraft station.

A New South Wales Fisheries station is on the southern shore where the research vessel Kapala is berthed.

There is a broad navigation channel near the mouth of the bay for the oil bunkers and the Fisheries jetty.

Gore Cove was named after William Gore, provost marshal under Governor Bligh, who was arrested along with Bligh during the infamous Rum Rebellion. Gore fared cruelly, being condemned to convict servitude till rescued and restored to office by Governor Macquarie.

GREENWICH

The tiny unnamed cove on the Greenwich peninsula, between Manns Point and Greenwich Point, is hardly the place to anchor, but like so many unlikely spots in the harbour, it has its

A tanker at Manns Point at the entrance to Gore Cove.

attractions despite the movement from passing vessels.

On the harbourside of Manns Point, which is a public reserve, is the Greenwich Sailing Club. There are a concrete launching ramps on either side of the club — the easterly ramp being for public use, the other for the club.

At the head of the bay are public baths. Tucked into the corner of the point — so tightly it is easily missed — is the Little Ship Slipway. Its twin slips can handle up to 30 tonnes. Harbour cruise boats and a dive boat are stationed there.

You can anchor beyond the moorings in the bay in good depth — about 5 metres — if you are prepared to tolerate some movement, particularly from harbour wakes. The advantage is the proximity of the ramps on the point — both sides of the yacht club — and it's a relative short walk from there to Manns Point Road, which becomes Greenwich Road.

Just beyond the cove, at the Greenwich Point end, is the Greenwich ferry wharf.

Clarkes Point

Clarkes Point marks the confluence of the Lane Cove River and the Parramatta River. Some regard it as the westernmost point of the harbour proper, though the writer believes that Pulpit Point to its west has a better claim, since Spectacle, Cockatoo and Snapper Island, plus Iron Cove should logically be included in the harbour.

The long, sweeping shoreline along the eastern aspect of Clarkes Point marks the mouth of the Lane Cove River.

The tip of Clarkes Point is a public reserve, which is surrounded by 7 hectares of military land, occupied by the 32nd Water Transport Squadron. The military has a 260 metre graving dock sliced out of the sandstone foreshore on the eastern side of the point to service its vessels, largely landing craft.

With the Transport Squadron due to move to Townsville at the end of 1997, the army is to dispose of the land. This triggered a local outcry from those who wanted the land converted to public reserve rather than sold off for development. What made this inevitable conflict especially newsworthy was that the land falls within the electorate of the Prime Minister, Mr Howard, and the locals were at pains to remind him.

FROM WALSH BAY TO BIRKENHEAD POINT ALONG THE SOUTHERN SHORE

WALSH BAY

Walsh Bay is the first past the Sydney Harbour Bridge — flanked by Dawes Point and Millers Point — on the southern shoreline. It is dominated by four pier wharves that once served international shipping. But the timber wharves, built at the turn of the century, face an uncertain future.

The NSW governments preferred tenderers, Mirvac and Transfield have suggested demolishing two of the wharves because of their poor state of repair. Parts are infested with termites.

But a report commissioned by the New South Wales government by Paris architect, Philippe Robert, who refurbished the historic Nestle building there, suggested the following for the 200-metre long Walsh bay wharves.

Pier 1: Application before the New South Wales government for a $40 million four star hotel complex.

Pier 2 & 3: Should be restored for cultural and public use, such as an art gallery.

Wharf 4 & 5: Should be restored. The Sydney Theatre company likely to remain there.

Wharf 6 & 7: This single storey wharf was described as the least significant of the wharves and could be demolished for a modern structure including apartments.

Wharf 8 & 9: To remain and be refurbished for either loft-style apartments or a boutique hotel.

The working end of Darling Harbour : the dock, from Millers Point.

It remains to be seen how the government responds to the report. But like Wooloomooloo, not much seems to be being done to diminish the apetitites of a lot of very well-fed wood borers.

As far as recreational boating is concerned, the issue is somewhat academic. No vessel is permitted to come alongside or anchor in the vicinity of the wharves and no marine services are mentioned in the report for the government.

Wharves which once bustled with whalers, cargo carriers and migrant ships from distant ports, their sailors carousing in The Rocks area, are to form the foundation of gentrified cultural pursuits and boutique accommodation — neat, clean and absolutely nothing marine other than water views.

GOAT ISLAND

Goat island, off Balmain, is about a kilometre upstream from the harbour bridge. The 5.5 hectare island, which rises to some 40 metres, was first used to graze goats then, in the 1830s, as a sandstone quarry and an arsenal.

The original buildings on the island, which still stand, are of particular historical significance. They were built by re-offending convicts, one of whom — "Bony" Anderson — was so incorrigible that he was chained by the neck to a sandstone outcrop for two years. Despite this inhuman restraint, he chipped away the sandstone to shape a seat for himself that survives today.

Fears for the city's safety eventually led to the dispersement of the explosives kept on the island, which was subsequently converted to a medical research station to combat the bubonic plague when it broke out in Sydney in 1900. Thereafter it gradually assumed a maritime purpose, engaged in the shipbuilding and repair of Sydney Harbour vessels of every description, from tugs to ferries.

It no longer serves a maritime function. Its future is not clear but one can only hope that it will become part of the Sydney Harbour National Parks.

An ideal solution would be the preservation of the original buildings and the restoration of at least that part of the island built in the convict period, though this would seem to be unlikely in view of the cost, not to mention the value of the real estate.

DARLING HARBOUR

Beyond Millers Point is the entrance to Darling Harbour, which extends in a southerly direction. (Do not be confused by the opening on the western side about half a kilometre inside the harbour: this leads to Johnstons Bay, on to White Bay, Blackwattle Bay and Rozelle Bay.)

Darling Harbour, to the writer, has a certain charm but suffers from a crisis of identity. It is an excellent harbour whose only reason for existence is now entertainment, recreation, conventions, eating, gambling, and any kitsch that will catch the tourist dollar, all of which is reasonable enough. But it has nothing to do with what this excellent harbour was so obviously designed for, that is, maritime activity.

The shipping wharves that line the eastern shores from Millers Point are suitably maritime, if rarely occupied by tonnage of any consequence. Between the docks and the Pyrmont Bridge is the National Aquarium and a ferry/cruise boat terminal. But the head of the harbour, which terminates in the perfect docking precinct of Cockle Bay, has all the maritime bustle and purpose of an ornamental pond.

The Sydney Harbour Casino occupies the prime pier at the approach to Cockle Bay and Foxtel another. The splendid Australian Maritime Museum — adjacent to the Pyrmont Bridge — with its fine display, including a Russian submarine, HMAS *Vampire* and others, is the saving grace of Darling Harbour from a maritime viewpoint. Certainly most of its ships are only for show, but without the museum, the area would be bereft indeed. It is to be hoped that the *James Craig*, once the museum has restored her, will be returned to Cockle Bay to add its maritime flavour. It may be too much to hope that splendid replica of the *Endeavour* may one day find her ideal home berth there.

Inside the Pyrmont bridge, now a walkway, with

Darling Harbour, looking towards the National Aquarium and ferry and cruise boat wharves. Pyrmont Bridge is on the right.

the sleek overhead monorail bussing in tourists, the harbour is reduced to an attractive pond to set off the rather glittering buildings of the convention centre with its backdrop of tourist hotels. It needs a maritime purpose; it needs vessels and it needs activity. Certainly it is crowded with vessels at the annual boat show — but that's another static display.

Perhaps this yearning for a maritime element is unrealistic. It may even be unfair, especially when one reflects on the ugly marshalling yards that the Darling Harbour complex replaced in the 1980s.

It is not as if there are no vessels at all in the area. There is a ferry and harbour cruise terminal at the finger wharves alongside the Aquarium, which can become quite busy. For this reason visiting vessels must keep to the right of the fairway when entering Darling Harbour — and observe the 8 knot zone beyond Millers Point and the no wash zone within the harbour itself.

The Pyrmont Bridge has a headway of 7.4 metres when closed and a span of 9 metres. The bridge is only raised for special events, so yachts cannot enter Cockle Bay. Those vessels that can, may moor alongside the seawall in daylight hours. The broad walkways around the complex are attractive and when it comes to variety, there are a variety of excursions for visitors, including the Chinese Gardens, the truly remarkable Powerhouse Museum, the Imax theatre with a screen more than 10 stories tall, and a choice of fast food outlets, restaurants and bars.

POINT PEACOCK

Vessels wishing to enter Johnstons Bay, White Bay, Blackwattle Bay and Rozelle Bay must turn west from Darling Harbour about half a kilometre past Millers Point.

Inside Point Peacock is a perfect little gem of an

Inside Point Peacock — "a perfect little gem.'

anchorage. It is a tiny little cove on the eastern side of Balmain. Only a few hectares in area it cannot accommodate many, but it is protected in all weathers. There is a sea wall all round, with steps at its head for easy shore access. It has 5 metres depth and good holding ground.

WHITE BAY

This bay, an offshoot of Johnsons Bay, is one of the few active shipping docks in the harbour. It is Sydney Harbour's major container terminal, largely for motor vehicles.

JOHNSONS BAY

There is nothing to recommend Johnsons Bay other than as an approach to Blackwattle and Rozelle Bays, which run east and west from the narrows at its head.

There, the old Glebe Island traffic bridge, with its limited access, was partially dismantled with the completion of the new Glebe Island Bridge. Three sections of the old bridge were left standing leaving two access ways of around 8 metres. Perhaps the old bridge has historical value to some, but it is not a pretty sight and it is strange that parts of it should remain to restrict the lateral opening when the costly new bridge opened-up so much height.

The new bridge rises from the disorder of this industrial waterfront area like a perfect web —

clean, precise, and exquisitely geometric. It is a truly beautiful bridge and it is of sufficient height — 27 metres — to allow all to pass.

Keep to the starboard side opening when entering the bay.

BLACKWATTLE AND ROZELLE BAYS

These two bays are grouped because they are really two arms of the same waterway. Rozelle Bay has a parklands beyond the sea wall along its southern shores, which provide agreeable shore access. Its northern wharves are occupied with marine activity.

There's about 5 metres depth along the northern banks and around 3 metres on the southern. Amongst the maintenance work conducted along the wharf on the on the northern banks is the restoration of historic ships for the Australian Maritime Museum. At the time of writing this included the *John Oxley, Kumala* and *Kanagra* ferries and the Tasmanian clipper *James Craig*. The long term plan for the area is to phase out industry and replace it with public facilities and private moorings.

Blackwattle Bay is east of the bridge. A pleasant anchorage can be found in the southern corner of this bay, off the Pioneer Concrete loading dock, and south of the rowing sheds. The Fishing Co-op is at the head of the bay and it's possible to hang off the jetty and go ashore for fresh fish or a meal at the local cafes.

Blackwattle Bay and Roselle Bay offer protection from all weather, flat waters and pleasant anchorages. They are, of course, in a metropolitan setting and if your delights are for natural surroundings this may not be your bag at all. But these bays have an authentic maritime atmosphere about them with the fishing fleet coming and going and the wharves active.

These bays might be among the very last harbour spots to contemplate swimming but they make a pleasant change when cruising — and they're calm.

MORT BAY

This is not a recommended anchorage. There is

Below: Fishing wharf at Blackwattle Bay.

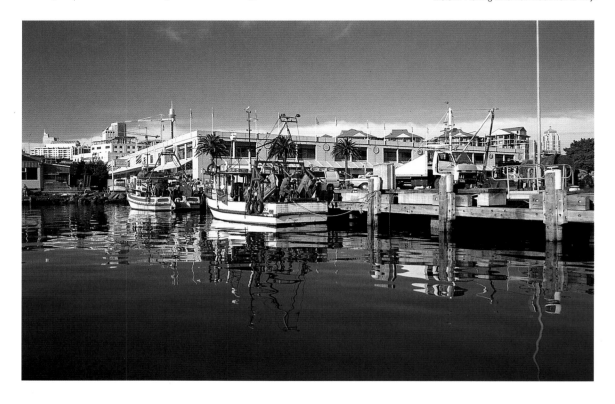

Rozelle Bay, a calm sanctuary dominated by the elegant web of the the new bridge.

too much movement, too many moorings, and the outlook is not particularly interesting, though there are tug and ferry docks at the head. If you have the mind to anchor, there is sufficient of depth and the best aspect is in the northeast corner of the bay.

There is also a small reserve on the southeastern shores of the bay.

SNAILS BAY

Snails Bay, protected by Long Nose Point on its western arm, is notable for the 15 mooring dolphins off its shores, which are used to transship cargo. Moorings and private jetties are strung along most of its shoreline, which is usually disturbed.

The Ballast Point arm is dominated by Caltex Oil. If a landing is needed, a small public park near Ballast Point offers shore access.

The most attractive part of the bay is inside Long Nose Point, where Birchgrove Park provides suitable landing opportunities, despite the sea wall.

There are anchoring possibilities beyond the moorings, and sufficient depth but movement must be expected.

The park there is also home to the Birchgrove Sabot Sailing Club, and tucked into the corner of this western end of the bay is Banks Marine. Its slipway can accommodate vessels up to 50 tonnes and it offers a variety of marine services, though not fuel.

COCKATOO ISLAND

Cockatoo Island lies at the mouth of the Parramatta River, midway between the shores of Woolwich and Birchgrove. The future of this 16 hectare sandstone island — like that of Goat Island — remained uncertain at the time of writing, though both islands brim with conservation possibilities — both good and bad.

Meantime, Cockatoo presents a melancholy sight to those who remember it as the powerhouse of heavy marine industry on the harbour. Its idle

cranes, silent workshops, and deserted wharves, seem frozen in time.

Visitors are not allowed on the Island and anchoring in its vicinity is prohibited.

Once a thickly wooded island with abundant birdlife, it was first called Bird Island on the earliest charts. (Cockatoos were eaten by early settlers to supplement their uncertain diet.) It had changed to Cockatoos Island by the 1830s, when a prison for some of the colony's worst convicts was established there.

The island soon earned a reputation for brutality, but the colony's first wheat silos where cut into its sandstone by its convict prisoners. Always the subject of controversy, it briefly became a women's prison and a refuge of sorts for homeless children before the government decided to develop the island into a shipbuilding yard prior World War 1. It remained so till its closure. The huge Sutherland and Fitzroy dry docks, now empty, accommodated some of the biggest ships to visit Sydney, from square-riggers to modern ocean liners. Cockatoo Island also built many fighting ships for the Royal Australian Navy, the largest of which was HMAS *Success*.

The closure of Cockatoo Island and loss of the jobs it entailed, shocked Sydneysiders. The loss was symbolic, highlighting a trend that shows all levels of maritime activity on Sydney Harbour diminishing, as the harbour drifts ever closer to the prophetic "pond in a private paddock".

It is to be hoped that the remains of the earliest prison buildings there can be restored and preserved. How much of the shipyard and dry dock facilities can be practicably kept is in the hands of the future owners — after the government has disposed of it.

SPECTACLE ISLAND

Lying to the west of Cockatoo Island is Spectacle Island, a Royal Australian Navy Armaments Depot. Anchoring in its precincts is strictly forbidden. In fact, the many warning signs displayed forbid

vessels from even "loitering" within 100 metres. Dolphins, between which are berthed ferro-cement armament lighters, lie to the north and south of the island. These concrete barges are designed with very heavy sides and light bases, so that any explosion would be directed downward. Navigate with due caution in this area (and note the numerous submarine cables).

Spectacle Island was first called Dawes Island, after the Second Lieutenant William Dawes of HMS *Sirius*. This was subsequently changed to Spectacle because of the shape of the island. It lay largely undisturbed till 1863, when it was developed as a powder magazine and taken over by the navy.

SNAPPER ISLAND

This tiny island, between Cockatoo Island, Spectacle Island and Birkenhead Point, is used by the navy as a training depot. Anchoring in its precincts is forbidden.

Balmain foreshore

The western shoreline of Birchgrove on the Balmain peninsula reflects the preferred lifestyle of the suburb theses (and the high cost of waterfront real estate). There are veritable walls of Mediterranean-style townhouses along this stretch, many with their own mooring pens at the doorstep. It is an attractive foreshore, the scale of the residential development seeming appropriate for its position in the harbour, at least to the writer. It is worth passing, if only to envy the locals their boating facilities. It highlights the demographic change to Balmain, once a fiercely proud traditional working class suburb, particularly for those of the shipbuilding and engineering trades that were, for over a century, the focus of industry in Balmain. Part of that rich tradition included Balmain's a long-lasting romance with watersports of all kinds, especially sculling, sailing and competitive swimming.

Sommerville Point

Sommerville Point marks the entrance to Iron Cove. The bay between Sommerville Point and

Opposite: Looking back across Longnose Point (Birchgrove) to towards Goat Island, Darling Harbour and the city skyline.

White Horse Point is a marine centre, one of the few that survives along the Balmain Peninsula. There is little possibility of anchoring.

IRON COVE

(See also Sisters Bay, King George Park, Rodd Island, Rodd Point)

Iron Cove, on the southern shores of the harbour, opens on to the mouth of the Parramatta River in the lee of Cockatoo and Spectacle Islands Its entrance is marked by Birkenhead Point (west) and Sommerville Point (east). This is a remarkably calm, but shallow waterway, its flat waters popular for rowing, canoeing and sailboarding.

The cove is about 500 metres wide and 2.5 kilometres long. If your draft exceeds 2 metres then it is probably best avoided. To enter the major part of the cove you must pass beneath Iron Cove Bridge, which has a clearance height of 12.3 metres.

Drummoyne Rowing Club is a landmark in Sisters Bay, the first cove inside the bridge along the western banks.

Further south is Half Moon Bay, but stand off some 70 metres from the shoreline once past the Half Moon Bay Yacht Club, because the depth shoals suddenly to about a metre.

Rodd Island — a tiny cultivated island about midstream — is a rare delight in Sydney Harbour.

Housing lines most of the bay but a green verge between the water and the foreshore road offers shore access practically anywhere.

The fact that there are four rowing clubs in Iron Cove gives some idea how flat the water is on the bay. This is not a place for carefree sailing in a keelboat, it's too shallow in parts, particularly in the bays on both sides of Rodd Point. But it is certainly navigable, if not to the shoreline, and the holding ground is excellent.

You need to be cautious of submarine cables anywhere near Rodd Island, where a number of cables cross. Watch out too for the collapsed seawall on the point south of the bridge, just beyond the moorings in the first bay on the eastern shore.

SISTERS BAY

Sisters Bay is the first bay beyond the bridge, near its northwestern end. It offers extremely quiet waters; it is free of moorings; is 2 to 3 metres deep; and has good holding ground. It also offers handy shore access (if a bit muddy at low tide) to the Drummoyne Rowing Club, Birkenhead Marina and its shop, and the Drummoyne shopping centre. It is best to favour the western shore of the bay to keep well clear of rowing club activity.

Brett Park, with barbecue facilities, dominates the head of the bay.

KING GEORGE PARK

The unnamed bay opposite Sisters Bay — that is, at the eastern end of the Iron Cove Bridge — has a number of moorings, but the advantage of good depth and the green sweep of King George Park behind it. Shore access (sea wall) is reasonably easy and the shops of Rozelle are not far away.

RODD ISLAND

Near the middle of Iron Cove lies tiny Rodd Island, part of the Sydney Harbour National Park. Visitors must make prior arrangements with National Parks and Wildlife. It is a charming spot with shelters, toilets and a public jetty on the southern tip. (Note the submarine cables.)

The island, beautifully maintained, is part of the Sydney Harbour National Park. The boating public, however, may not land there without prior permission from the authority.

Though there are undoubtedly reasonable arguments for the enforcement of such regulations, it seems a shame that visiting such reserves is so actively discouraged. "Prior permission" removes all the joy of a chance encounter, quite apart from it being an irritation to the independent spirit of boating and exploring.

Is the boating fraternity so irresponsible that it cannot be trusted without supervision? Is the bureaucracy too authoritarian in its exercise? Is a majority being penalised because a minority might misbehave? Or is the real agenda to discourage people from visiting these reserves if you cannot enlist sufficient public support to ban them completely?

To the writer, at least, none of the foregoing possibilities are compelling. Boating is a whimsical, spontaneous pastime. It is rarely planned, being dependent on the weather, the company, and even the mood of the moment. That's the nub of its carefree appeal. Arranging prior permission is an antithesis. Harbour development, ignoring its worthiness or its legitimacy, has already denied the harbour to too many Sydneysiders in too many places. So it is always encouraging when the political will is marshalled to create public reserves. To then severely limit the public access to these reserves — and "prior permission" is certainly discouragement if not denial — is very difficult to cheer about.

Rodd Island has a curious history. In 1888, the great microbiologist Louis Pasteur responded to a 25,000-pound prize for a biological method of reducing the rabbit plague in Australia, and Rodd Island was chosen as an experimental centre. To Pasteur's chagrin, his microbiological solution was rejected because of its indiscriminate effects on native bird life. The island was later used by Pasteur' Institute to produce an anthrax vaccine.

Public opinion reclaimed the island for public use in 1894. It became a popular picnic and dance destination from the 1920s to the 1960s. Briefly leased to a marina company, it was reclaimed again, this time for the National Parks and Wildlife to administer as part of the Sydney Harbour National Park.

RODD POINT

Rodd Point divides the head of Iron Cove into a double bay. The bays on both sides are very shallow but this pleasant headland reserve is easily reached by dinghy.

Birkenhead Point

Birkenhead Point at the tip of the Drummoyne peninsula is the site of the Birkenhead Marina and shopping complex, and Drummoyne Sailing Club.

Birkenhead Marina, with 200 berths, is one of the largest on the harbour. It also offers short term berths for visitors, though it is best to call in advance. If not, pull alongside the fuelling berth to make enquiries. Anchoring off Birkenhead Point is certainly not a realistic option.

Remarkably, the marina does not have a slipway, but it does sell fuel — both diesel and petrol — and ice. Its special advantage is the shopping complex in the old factory buildings behind it, which includes a wide variety of the shops and cafes. Further, it offers access to Victoria Road.

If you need to land a dinghy, it is best managed nearer the Drummoyne Sailing Club, west of the marina. The club welcomes visitors to its restaurant, bar, and bistro.

LANE COVE RIVER

FUEL : NONE

PUBLIC LAUNCHING RAMPS : WOOLWICH, BURNS BAY

THE river is one of the most pleasant cruising destinations on the harbour. Though its banks are largely lined with private homes, the absence of overbearing blocks of units or industrial/commercial activity, and the pleasing scale of the waterfront landscape makes it attractive. The river's flat water and comparitive freedom from commercial traffic completes the picture. Well, almost.

On the downside, the riverbanks are lined with moorings, making it difficult to find an anchorage, the Fig Tree bridge has a clearance of only 9.1 metres, limiting the upstream progress for yachts, and cruise boats disturb the evening's reverie if you are overnighting, particularly on weekends.

There's no doubt this waterway is best suited to smaller vessels, because of the limited room and depths. But if you plan your sojourn there carefully, it is a very pleasant indeed, particularly daycruising. Like so much of the harbour, it is best on week days. And best of all on sunny winters days.

ENTRANCE

The breeze at the entrance to Lane Cover River, influenced by the headlands of Greenwich and Woolwich, is notoriously flukey for the sailing vessel.

Though this would surprise no-one, becalmed skippers should be concious of the ferries that have right of way, both to Bay Street and Northwood wharves inside the entrance and the Valentia Street wharf at the entrance. In other words, you may need the motor. (Locals call this fickle zone the Humbug.)

There are moorings along both banks, but on the southern banks — inside Greenwich Point — there is a pleasant strip of parkland with small sandy beaches to land a dinghy. From here you can gain access to Church Street and Greenwich Road if need be.

This area is reasonably protected from most breezes, though it gets bumpy from time to time from passing traffic, particularly ferries.

Onions Point

Onions Point marks the hub of the sharp bend the river takes from its northeasterly path at the entrance to a westerly tendency thereafter.

It offers no navigation hazard, unless you regard a few moorings that seriously, and it is noted here for no other reason than the writer's indulgence. I regard it the prettiest developed point on the harbour. Such views are subjective, but the scale seems appropriate and homes blend well with their surroundings.

Many times the writer has passed Onion Point and reflected enviously on the waterfront lifestyle of those that live there. Taking tea or a glass of wine, or rustling up a barbecue in the green shade of those gardens on a warm summer's evening, the river a sheet of glass broken only by the wake of a homecoming yacht... Surely, bliss.

NORTHWOOD POINT (unnamed)

Opposite Onion Point is an unamed point, dominated by the Northwood Ferry wharf. On its eastern side is a tiny unamed cove with around 5 metres at the entrance, 3 metres about half way in and 2 metres at the head, where is shoals suddenly to mud flats. There is precious little space for mooring let alone anchoring and should not be considered for more than a brief stopover. Shore access for the dinghy can be made at the small reserve just inside Northwood Wharf. You can climb the grassy slopes of park to street level.

WOODFORD BAY

This bay, opposite Onions Point, flanked by Northwood and Longueville, is by far the biggest on the Lane River. It is also as crowded as any on the harbour and cannot be recommended for anchorage.

The patient cruiser will, however, find a few spots around the fringes for smaller boats on a necessarily short scope, but it could not be seriously contemplated in fresh winds.

There is a launching ramp just inside the bay's most western Longueville point (unnamed), with access to Dunios Street. A dinghy can be readily beached on the small reserve there.

Another landing point is in the northernmost corner at the head of the bay, which offers access to Woodford Street.

The depth, in most of the bay, is around the 3-metre mark but don't approach the shore too closely, particularly the northern shore.

SOUTHERN BANKS (Woolwich)

The long sweep of the southern banks of the river — between Onions Point and Alexandra Bay and Onions Point — is largely lined with moorings. Access to handy streets is limited. But there is a spot that could serve as at least a temporary anchorage about half way along this stretch. It is free of moorings, with around 2 metres depth about 30 metres offshore. It has a pleasant outlook too. There are two tidal pools nearby to the east with sandy beaches for easy dinghy landing and street access to Woolwich Road and the nearby Woolwich Hotel. Further along, Gale Street terminates at the waters' edge, though a seawall there makes landing awkward.

ALEXANDRA BAY

This bay is a large bite that marks the end of the broad navigable reaches of the river, which narrow markedly past Newcombe Point. The southern heights are part of the Woolwich Peninsular which is one of the harbour's dress circle suburbs. The bay is quite crowded with moorings but, provided you keep clear of the navigation channel (particularly to the Alexandra Street ferry wharf) it is possible to squeeze in, though it is not recommended unless you particularly enjoy the charming real estate views. The public wharf inside Newcombe point here is closed to all vessels between 6am and 6pm.

YACHT BAY

Opposite Alexandra Bay, this small cove is packed

An attractive aspect of Alexandra Bay on the Lane Cove River.

tight with moorings. The Lane Cove 12 Foot Sailing Club and the North Shore Rowing Club are situated on is eastern headland, Butchers Block Point. If you can find a spot, there is up to 3 metres depth and good holding mud, though it is not recommended for anything other than a temporary stop.

TAMBOURINE BAY

This is a delightful little bay, the head of which is lined with mangroves. It is fairly crowded with about 30 moorings, most of which lie in about 2 metres. Inside the fringe of the moorings, the waters shoals from 1-plus metres and less. The mud dries at the head at low tide.

It is, nevertheless, a charming and protected anchorage is you can squeeze in somewhere on a short scope.

St Ignatius College (Riverview), founded 1880 occupies the western headland but there are public reserves at the head of the bay, notably Hodgson Park and there's a small tidal pool on the northern shore. Riverview, Macquarie University and the Sea Scouts have rowing sheds in the bay.

According to historian P.R. Stephenson, the bay was named after a notorious woman known as Tambourine Nell who hid there for some time in the vain hope that she would avoid the arm of the law.

BURNS BAY

The river is extremely shallow beyond Tambourine Bay, so proceed upriver with caution. Leaving Tambourine Bay to starboard, hug the port marks, which tend to the northern shore. Hold this course till the last port mark near the mouth of Burns Bay, where two white, triangular lead markers (small reflective red triangles mounted in the centre) will come into view at the foot of Linley Point on the eastern side of the bay.

Once you have these aligned, proceed across the mouth of the bay till adjacent with the line of moored boats: turn into the bay, close to the line of moorings, and you can proceed to the head of the bay, keeping well clear of the banks, which shoal to mud.

Anchoring is difficult but there are occasionally a couple of spots at the head of the bay. Otherwise, anchor at the mouth, keeping clear of the channel.

This is a very pretty. well-protected bay, with Burns Bay Reserve a pleasant enough landing spot (a launching ramp in the northwest corner is easiest). Alternatively there is a grassy fringe on the opposite banks, though it's a little rocky. It's a steep walk to River Road and a very long walk to the nearest shops at Lane Cove.

Large blocks of units dominate the head of the bay — bliss to be looking out from but not quite so uplifting to look at! On the western side are private homes to the water's edge. The peak of the eastern headland is dominated by St Ignatius College, better known as Riverview.

UPPER LANE COVE RIVER

The river upstream of Burns Bay is limited to vessels that can pass under Figtree Bridge, with a clearance of 9.1 metres. From there the river tends north and narrows markedly beyond Linley Point. The narrow channel, with mangroves along both banks is well-marked with beacons.

Frankly, it not worth the effort for deep draughted vessels and few yachts of larger than, say, 7 metres overall will pass under Fig Tree Bridge to get that far.

The Mowbray Road Footbridge has a 9.4 metres clearance but overhead cables become an increasing problem if you proceed. The Epping Road Bridge with a clearance of 6.4 metrers and Fuller Bridge, with 4.4 metres creates further problems. The best solution is to anchor downstream of Figtree bridge and take the dinghy and outboard upstream — then it is worth the effort without the worry.

PARRAMATTA RIVER

FUEL : BIRKENHEAD POINT, FIVE DOCK POINT, CABARITA POINT

PUBLIC LAUNCHING RAMPS : CLARKES POINT, FIVE DOCK BAY, CABARITA POINT, KISSING POINT, RHODES POINT

THE Parramatta River is often overlooked if not ignored by harbour users. Yet despite it more fitful breezes, the result of more confined waters, it has the advantage of flat water for cruising and anchoring, qualities not lost on the rowing fraternity, which abound along its reaches.

The area is also fragrant with Australian history. Governor Phillip intended to make Parramatta, with its better soil for agriculture, the capitol of New South Wales. He built Government House there in 1790. But the ease of access to Sydney Cove compared with the difficulty of sailing upriver was among the reasons that the Parramatta option was never realised. It must be remembered that the waterways provided the most effective communications and transport link for the community right up to this century. It was critical in the first hundred years.

Parramatta was called Rose Hill when it was first farmed within months of First Settlement. It was renamed Parramatta in 1791, which is believed to mean "place where eels lie down" in the Aboriginal language, though "head of river" is another interpretation. It is one of few places on the harbour — indeed in Sydney — that preserved its Aboriginal place-name, which in hindsight seems a pity. It is not unreasonable, however, to sympathise with the colonists for clinging to familiar nomenclature to help demystifying the alien land around them. Any atlas of the previously colonised world shows it was a universal reaction — in any number of the languages of colonisation.

The Parramatta River offers more than a dozen bays, admittedly of varied depths. It shoreline, while generally flatter than that of the main harbour, is always interesting, particularly for those with a penchant for waterside architecture. And there are a remarkable number of waterfront reserves, though relatively small. There's never enough, of course, but more than generally believed and usually well-tended. This is not to deny that the river has some dreary pockets where industry or commerce is predominant. Homebush Bay springs readily to mind but there are others. Yet the mix creates variety and interest, all essential elements in a working metropolitan river. It has two particularly attractive bridges, the towering grandeur of the Gladesville Bridge and an almost miniature replica that crosses Tarban Creek.

Another advantage of this section of the harbour is the easier shore access to shops. The sleek rivercat ferries offer regular communication between Circular Quay and Silverwater.

The scope of this book ends at Silverwater Bridge.

The river officially starts beyond Long Nose Point and Clarkes Point, though Pulpit Point and Birkenhead Point would seem more logical, leaving Cockatoo, Snapper and Spectacle islands, plus Iron Cove in the harbour.

PARRAMATTA RIVER
GLADESVILLE BRIDGE TO RYDE BRIDGE

RYDE

Launch ramp access
via: Delange Road

Victoria Road

Higginbotham Road

Church Street

Morrison Road

RYDE BRIDGE
(11.8m)

Charles Street

Delange Road

GLADESVILL

KISSING
POINT
PARK
PARK

Morrison Road

PUTNEY

MORRISON
BAY PARK

TENNYSON

Brays
Bay

Kissing Point

FISHERS
MARINA

moorings

Morrison
Bay

Tennyson Road

Rocky Point

Kissing
Point Bay

Pellisser Road

Putney Point

Raven Point

Glades
Bay

Yaralla
Bay

Mortlake Point   Hilly Street

moorings

moorings

Looking Glass Point

PARRAMATTA RIVER S.C.

Punt Road

Be

Looking
Glass Bay

Majors
Bay

Tennyson Road

Breakfast Point

MORTLAKE

PRIVATE
WHARF

Kendall
Bay

Cabarita
Point

WESTPORT
MARINA

ABBOTSFORD BOATSHED

ABBOTSFO

Hospital Road

RIVER QUAYS MARINA

PUNT CROSSING

Launch ramp
access via: Cabarita Park
at end Cabarita Road

BATTERSEA
PARK

Great North

WALKER
RESERVE

Gale Street

CABARITA

Cabarita Road

moorings

moorings

France Bay

Mortlake Street

CONCORD

Cabarita Road

Phillips Street

Hen
and
Chicken
Bay

Whymson Parade

MASSEY PARK
GOLF COURSE

moorings

Exile Bay

Reg

Launch ramp access
via: Bay View Park at end
Burwood Road

BAY
VIEW
PARK

Burwood Road

Canada Bay

GOLF
COURSE

Crane Street

Kings
Bay

CANADA
BAY

Lyons

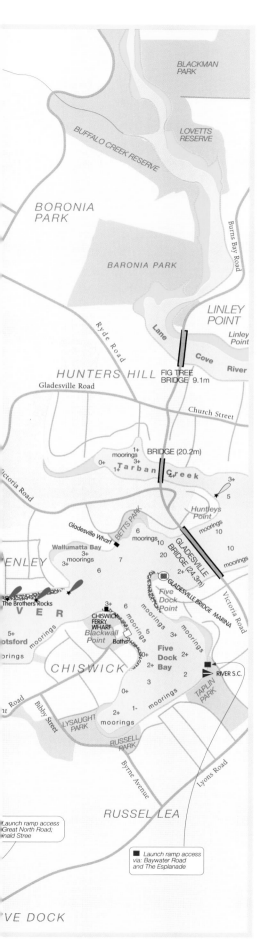

There is little that need concern cruising vessels. There is minimal tide or current of consequence and even the shoal ground found at the head of most bays is invariably mud. If you keep clear of the navigation channels, particularly in the (upper) narrower sections of the river, and remain conscious that submarine cables cross the river, it can be rewarding and tranquil cruising, particularly in the winter months.

DRUMMOYNE

A long seawall follows the southern shore from Birkenhead Point towards Drummoyne Point, behind which is a seemingly endless wall of flats and a few homes. (Note the submarine cables to Spectacle Island.)

Once past the President's Boatshed and the Allcraft Slipway there is about 2 metres depth some 30 metres off the sea wall and more depth beyond, but it is prudent to pass outside the mooring line. There's a particularly shallow patch about half way along the wall — between the two submarine cable signs.

Anchoring along this strip cannot be recommended. The moorings are crowded and its quite busy in commercial hours. And the waters that surround Spectacle Island, off this shoreline, are naval waters in which even loitering is discouraged and anchoring forbidden.

DRUMMOYNE BAY

The Drummoyne Wharf stands on the southern point of this bay where there's a public telephone. The bay itself is neat, relatively calm but innocuous, but it offers potential refuge in a southerly. There are moorings throughout but it's possible to anchor outside them, if cautious. Surrounded by high-rise units to the water's edge, the only shore access is a tiny reserve inside Wrights Point where you can land a dinghy — but it's a rocky landing.

⬤	MARINA WITH FUEL
■	MARINA
■	LAUNCHING RAMP
▶	YACHT CLUB
☐	RECREATIONAL AREAS
☐	STATE/NATIONAL PARKS
☐	SAND, USUALLY MUDDY
■	ROCKS
〜	MAJOR ACCESS
◀	STARBOARD NAV LIGHT/BEACON
◀	PORT NAV LIGHT/BEACON
◁	WHITE/YELLOW NAV LIGHT/BEACON
4k	MAXIMUM SPEED 4 KNOTS

FERN BAY

This bay is completely dominated by the huge Pulpit Point estate development, whose imposing private marina is tucked into the bight.. There is plenty of depth beyond the marina but the movement discourages anchorage.

East of Fern Bay is a small bulge in the shore-line, inside which — behind Kelly's Bush — is tucked the Woolwich Marina and its three slips.

East of the marina is a ramp and the Hunters Hill Sailing Club. You can anchor in good depth quite close in near the club but it's a little exposed and unsettled by passing traffic.

LUKES BAY

This cove offers no welcome to the cruising vessel, but it's worth a quick loop to admire the waterside homes and envy the private mooring facilities. There is a small strip of park just inside the western point with steps to the water and access to Woodward Road if a temporary stop is needed.

TARBAN CREEK

Steep cliffs walls the entrance to this inlet, one of the more charming little waterways in Sydney Harbour. The wind does whistle though this cutting, particularly when there's some east in it, but the water is quite flat.

A road bridge of 20 metres clearance — like a miniature of the Gladesville Bridge that it ultimately joins — straddles the inlet. There is a seawall at the head, where the muddy Tarban Creek empties into the cutting. The St Joseph's Rowing Club is situated at the head and the University of Sydney Rowing Club.

There is good water throughout this inlet though dense mooring along both shores makes anchoring difficult if not impossible.

Road access can be found in the northern corner, inside the bridge, where there is a tiny park — the track will take you to George Street.

GLADESVILLE BRIDGE

The lofty arc of Gladesville Bridge, 300 metres long and 24.3 metres above high water springs, spans the river between Drummoyne and Huntleys Point. It carries Victoria Road, a major western artery. When opened in December, 1964, it was the longest single arch concrete span in the world.

Moorings line both banks of the river at this point. It is not recommended as an anchorage.

Upriver of the bridge, along the northern shore, are the reserves of Betts Park and Gladesville Reserve. The unamed cove that abuts the latter — beyond the Gladesville ferry wharf — offers the best chance of a temporary anchorage, though the moorings could preclude this.

Anchoring on the southern side of the river in the vicinity of the bridge is out of the question.

Five Dock Point is the most prominent, rock landform, inside which (on the bridge side) is Gladesville Bridge Marina, which offers a range of marine service, including slipping and fuel. It also has a busy brokerage. There is a tiny reserve on the tip of Five Dock Point but the shores here a generally lined with housing, particularly apartments

The towering arch of Gladesville Bridge.

The century-old monument to world champion sculler, Henry Searle at Henley Point on the Parramatta River. Sydney produced a string of world champions in the mid 1800s.

FIVE DOCK BAY

The mouth, between Blackwall Point and rocky promontory of Five Dock Point, opens to a broad, relatively calm bay. There is some 2-plus metres depth in all but the head of the bay, which shoals inside the inner perimeter of the mooring line.

Mooring are set off most of the shoreline but there is room to anchor and plenty of parks ashore to visit. There is housing around all shores, apart from those areas occupied by Taplin Park on the eastern shore, the Campbell and Russell Parks at the head. The clean, sculptured arch of the Gladesville Bridge, dominates the eastern aspect. A sea wall the length of the eastern shore is broken only by a generously wide launching ramp at the foot of the broad sweep of Taplin Park.

The head of the bay shoals to mud but landing is easily managed at the three public parks.

Five Dock Bay — a bay which in fact had no docks — took its name from a local farm so-named by Irishman John Harris, who had arrived as an army surgeon in 1790. Governor King granted him a large parcel of land in the area in 1806.

ABBOTSFORD BAY

Blocks of units dominate the eastern banks of this bay; huge factories and warehouses dominate the head. It is not an ideal anchorage but it does offer protection in a southerly. Landings can be made on narrow reserve on eastern shore.

WALLUMATTA BAY

This steep-walled bay on the northern shores, opposite Five Dock Bay, is tiny but snug. The western shore is lined with private homes but the Gladesville Reserve is at the head of the bay. Vessels should keep clear of the shoreline. It shoals to around 2 metres and the bottom is quite rocky. The rocky shore in the northeast corner of the bay is the best place to land.

East of Wallumatta is another delightful little unamed cove, just upstream of the Gladesville Bridge, the head of which is Betts Park, where it is possible to land.

There is good depth in this little cove, but again it is prudent to be cautions of the rocky shoreline.

Henley Point

Opposing Abbotsford Bay is Henley Point, which is remarkable for The Brothers Rocks — large boulder-like rocks projecting from the point — which are well marked and lit.

Near the extremity of the rocks stands a charming, well-maintained monument to Henry Ernest Searle, who was the world sculling champion in 1888 and 1889. On the voyage home from England, where he had successfully defended his world title against the American champion W.J. O'Connor, the popular 23-year-old was struck down by a fever and died of peritonitis.

Sculling had an enormous following in Sydney at the time. Then a professional sport for a purse, much like boxing, it attracted enormous crowds and serious wagers on the outcome. It was the most popular sport in Sydney for much of the 1800s — from 1847 when the first race was held. Ted

The swift, sleek rivercats with minimal wake.

Trickett, Australia's first recognised world champion in any sport, had already won the world crown in 1876 in England.

Some 250,000 turned out to pay their respects to Searle when his coffin was returned home via Sydney. A public subscription was raised and the broken column memorial was erected on The Brothers Rocks in 1891.

LOOKING GLASS BAY

Though the bay is cluttered with moorings it is well worth the effort. A delightful place to anchor is off Banjo Paterson Park, which has a substantial jetty and access to the historic Banjo Paterson Restaurant. The sandstone restaurant was once the home of Australia's best-known and best-loved poet, Andrew Barton "Banjo" Paterson (1864-1941), who not only idealised the bush in his enormously popular ballads but immortalised Waltzing Matilda, now a sentimental anthem that tugs the strings of Australian hearts like no other, whenever it is heard.

There is also a tiny sand/mud beach from which access may be gained to Bernard street and hence Wharf Road (Gladesville).

HEN AND CHICKEN BAY

This is a large, shallow, estuarine inlet with low-lying shores, scads of room and depths of around 2-plus metres.

There are, of course, plenty of moorings in the bay but there is room for all with the added advantage of an absence of commercial traffic

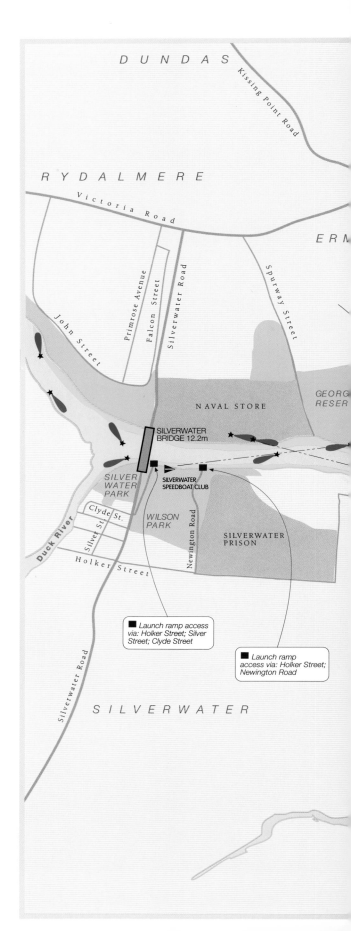

MARINA WITH FUEL
MARINA
LAUNCHING RAMP
YACHT CLUB
RECREATIONAL AREAS
STATE/NATIONAL PARKS
SAND, USUALLY MUDDY
ROCKS
MAJOR ACCESS
STARBOARD NAV LIGHT/BEACON
PORT NAV LIGHT/BEACON
WHITE/YELLOW NAV LIGHT/BEACON
4k   MAXIMUM SPEED 4 KNOTS

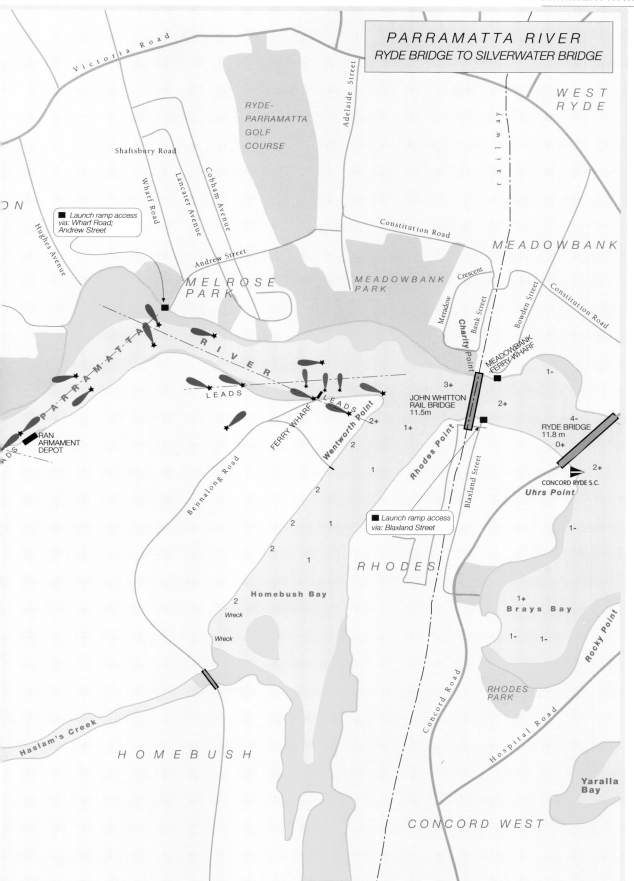

PARRAMATTA RIVER
RYDE BRIDGE TO SILVERWATER BRIDGE

WEST RYDE

Victoria Road

Shaftsbury Road

RYDE-PARRAMATTA GOLF COURSE

Adelaide Street

railway

MEADOWBANK

Wharf Road

Lancaster Avenue

Cobham Avenue

Constitution Road

Andrew Street

Hughes Avenue

Launch ramp access via: Wharf Road; Andrew Street

MELROSE PARK

MEADOWBANK PARK

Crescent

Meadow Street

Bank Street

Bowden Street

Constitution Road

PARRAMATTA RIVER

Charity Point

MEADOWBANK FERRY WHARF

1-

LEADS

FERRY WHARF

LEADS

Wentworth Point

3+

JOHN WHITTON RAIL BRIDGE 11.5m

2+

1-

RAN ARMAMENT DEPOT

2+

1+

4-

RYDE BRIDGE 11.8 m

0+

2

Rhodes Point

CONCORD RYDE S.C.

2+

Bennalong Road

1

Blaxland Street

Uhrs Point

2

2

1

Launch ramp access via: Blaxland Street

1-

2

1

RHODES

2

Homebush Bay

1+

Brays Bay

2

Wreck

Concord Road

1-

1-

Rocky Point

Wreck

RHODES PARK

Haslam's Creek

Hospital Road

HOMEBUSH

Yaralla Bay

CONCORD WEST

to stir up unwelcome wakes. The ground, being mud/sand, offers excellent holding.

A further advantage is the easy access to roads, particularly Wymston Parade, which skirts most of the eastern shoreline. And there are some eight reserves of varying sizes on which to land for a picnic.

There are launching ramps too, on both sides of the bay: one midway along the eastern shore and another, almost opposite, on Bayview Park point.

On Cabarita Point stands the handsome Westport Marina offering most marine services, including fuel, and the park on the pont allows shore access to most parts.

Having lauded its many advantages, one is obliged to add that it is not one of the handsomest bays on the harbour in its setting. But it is pleasant, protected and comfortable.

The bights in the western shoreline of Hen and Chicken Bay are separately named (*see* entries). They are: Frances Bay, Exile Bay, Canada Bay and Kings Bay.

Three of these bays take their names from a group of French-Canadian political prisoners who were sent to Australia in 1840 after having been involved in an unsuccessful revolt against the crown in Canada. This was the very year that the transportation of convicts to New South Wales was finally stopped, largely because of Australian sensibilities. The governor of the time, Sir George Gipps, sensitive about the timing of the Canadian arrivals and the nature of their crime, treated them more as prisoners of war under military supervision at Hen and Chicken Bay. The prisoners were given a great deal of latitude and most were pardoned and returned to Canada a few years later.

The origins of the name, Hen and Chicken Bay, is not so well documented. Captain Hunter and Lieutenant Bradley explored Parramatta River in 1788, when the marshy flats of the inlet would have been surrounded by mangroves. One theory suggests that they noted that sandstone rocks near the entrance resembled a hen and chicken: the

other suggests that they sighted and emu and her chick there. Neither claim can be substantiated.

FRANCE BAY

This is so shallow bay that even shoal-draughted vessels need to proceed with some caution towards its head. It is not an ideal anchorage because of the depths and in any event, at the time of writing the outlook was dominated by massive sandstone mining at its head.

EXILE BAY

Like all the bays on the western shoreline of Hen and Chicken Bay, the waters here are shallow. Nevertheless it is possible to anchor at the mouth. The southern outlook is dominated by prominent new townhouses.

The reserve at the head of the bay is part of the Massey Park Golf Links and a seawall makes landing a dinghy awkward. If going ashore, it is best to beach near the ramp at Bay View Park on the southern point.

CANADA BAY

This is the shallowest of the bays within Hen and Chicken Bay, but it has a pleasant outlook for those with sufficiently shoal drafted vessels. The southern shores offer easy access to the road system and shops — a green verge lies between the waterfront and the road along the shore.

(The bay inside Bedlam Point has deeper water and moorings.) The shore in this area, however, is part of thehospital grounds.

KENDALL BAY

Upstream of Cabarita Point, Kendall Bay would be a perfect anchorage were it not for the unprepossessing dominance of a dilapidated factory on its steep western shore. It is a depressing eyesore, a bleak, disused and dilapidated brick structure of the Australian Gas Company, once one of the largest gas companies in the world, which has commanded the vast majority of the territory around Breakfast Point since 1888, including the

The Putney Ferry, a vehicular punt drawn across the river on wire ropes.

heavy jetty beneath the factory, used largely as a coal loader.

How very different Breakfast Point must have looked when it was named in 1788 by Captain Hunter and Lieutentant Bradley, who shared breakfast there with local Aborigines while charting the course of the Parramatta River?

If you can ignore the eyesore — which is not easy if you have an affection for this great waterway — the bay offers many attractions as a temporary anchorage, at least, particularly if your vessel is deep draughted. There is good, deep water in this little bay, unless you stray too close to Cabarita Point where is shoals to mud and rocks. And there are not many such deep bays on the river. Added to this is the pleasant little park on the tip of Cabarita Point itself, where it is easy to land. In fact, is has a launching ramp there.

There are two items of interest in Cabarita Park. One is the waterfront obelisk, which is a memorial to the 1884 world champion sculler, William Beach. The other is of more monumental historical significance: the pavilion in which Federation

was formally proclaimed in 1901. Though this event took place in Centennial Park, the ornate pavilion was subsequently moved to Cabarita Park.

GLADES BAY

Opposite Kendall Bay is the narrower Glades Bay, lined with splendidly well-established waterfront homes. There are many moorings in the bay, which has an average depth of around 2-plus metres but room can be found with a little care and discretion — a very tranquil anchorage.

MORRISON BAY

This is a pleasant, open bay, with good depth for this part of the harbour. Morrison Bay Park is at its head, beyond a seawall, but there are sufficient sand/mud patches to land a dinghy comfortably.

The southern outlook is blighted by the ugly abandoned factory of the Australian Gas Company, which must surely be demolished in time. A pleasing range of largely modern homes, right to the waterfront, enhance the landscape but other than that, this is a pleasant if unremarkable bay.

The arresting architecture of the Walker Convalescen Home at Rocky Point.

An extraordinary number of homes here enjoy private slipways, jetties and ramps — but not one for the public! The number of moorings discourages anchoring.

MORTLAKE

Rows of new townhouses, replete with jetty and private pens, mark the eastern aspect of Mortlake Point, beyond which is a tiny picnic park (on the tip of the point) with a formidably ponderous name — the Wangal Centenary Bushland Reserve. How do our civic fathers make such large mouthfuls for such modest meals?

A red beacon marks the extremity of the point.

The busy shoreline between Mortlake Point (west) and Breakfast Point (east) is usually referred to simply as Mortlake.

It is the site of River Quays Marina, opened in 1990, with a huge workshop and lifting cradle. Its facilities match any on the harbour and it can handle practically any marine work.

Adjacent to the marina is the vehicular punt — known locally as the Putney Ferry — which is drawn across the river by cables. It creates a navigation hazard that should not be taken lightly, even though it moves at a snail's pace. Once it starts moving, the cables rise under tension creating a trip wire across the river, especially for deep keels. It does not run often enough to be a nuisance but vessels should not attempt to cross its path once the ferry is under way. In fact, boats are required to reduce their speed to 4 knots within 100 metres of the ferry.

Mortlake could not be regarded as a pretty anchorage but it has good depth and holding ground. The most likely spot is east of the marina. Shore access is more of a problem. The best landing is a small stretch of beach west of the ferry (if you wish to walk to the Palace Hotel in Tennyson road or along the point to the reserve) or across the river at the Putney Point Reserve.

KISSING POINT BAY

Opposite Mortlake is Kissing Point Bay, which is more part of a natural bend in the river than a bay, It is flanked by Putney Point (east) and Kissing

Mangroves and rusting hulks dominate the head of shallow Homebush Bay.

Point (right) both which have pleasing reserves.

Putney Point is the northern shore terminal of the vehicular ferry — Pellisier Road — but its western aspect is part of pleasant Putney Park. Nevertheless, Kissing Point Park on the opposing point is probably a preferable landing place.

This reserve extends to the point and there is sufficient sand/mud along the shoreline to make a landing possible on this pleasant picnic ground. There is a concrete launching ramp at the end of Kissing Point.

This is not an ideal anchorage. Lack of seclusion, a shoaling head, and the activity on this part of the river being discouraging factors.

MAJORS BAY

Despite the industrial development around this part of the river, the mangroves that fringe the shallow, muddy heads of Majors Bay and Yaralla Bay — and, to a lesser extent, Brays Bay — remain critical for fish-breeding in the river ecosystem.

The eastern entrance to this double bay is not particularly inviting, with its largely industrial buildings and a small strip of townhouses along the eastern shore.

Vessels should stand off some 30 metres from the sea wall at the entrance — it shoals suddenly. The bay is really too shallow for boats with any sort of draught, but the most suitable anchorage seems to be off the point that divides the twin bays of Majors and Yaralla, with near 2 metres of water and a heavy mud bottom. This headland, however, is part of the Yaralla Hospital grounds.

Up till the inside line of moorings there is near 2 metres depth, thereafter it falls away to around the metre mark and only shoal draught vessels need proceed. In fact, beyond the moorings into the bay it is a pretty mangrove bay with a reserve beyond its head.

But go with care. Remember, fish are breeding!

YARALLA BAY

Narrow Yaralla Bay is really a western inlet of Majors Bay. Fringed with mangroves and free of moorings this is a pleasant anchorage, particularly for shoal-draughted vessels — despite some aspects

The rivercat ferry at the rail bridge adjacent to Home Bush Bay.

being dominated by smoke stacks and the Concord Repatriation Hospital.

(In view of its importance as a critical fish-breeding ground, it would not seem unreasonable to ban fishing and boating in its precincts.)

Depths, midway between the two points are about 3 metres , but if your draught allows it, tuck into the southern bight inside Rocky Point. There's only about 2 metres depth there but it's a charming anchorage if you can manage it.

Rocky Point

The most most remarkable feature of this point is the arresting structure of the Walker Convalescent Home and its delightful annexe at the water's edge, which dominates Rocky Point. The port-hand beacon is mounted on the riverside portal of the annexe, an elegant river landmark, clearly visible when approaching from either direction.

BRAYS BAY

This shallow, circular-shaped bay — often called

Horseshoe Bay — lies between Rocky Point (east) and Uhrs Point (west), with Rhodes Park and McIlwaine Parks at its head.

Though there is ample room in the bay for anchoring, the shores are muddy and the waters extremely shallow near the shore. If your draft exceeds 2 metres this is not the bay for you since its deepest parts — mid way between the two points — barely reaches 2 metres.

On the opposite shore of the river is the Australian Defence Industries establishment which, like so many waterfront industries, was up for sale at the time of writing. This marine complex that was formerly the warmly-remembered Halvorsens Boatyard.

RYDE BRIDGE (S)

The northerly bay between the Ryde Bridge (clearance 11.8 metres) and the Rhodes (rail) Bridge (clearance 11.5 metres) offers an uninspiring view but excellent protection and access to shops ashore.

There is also a launching ramp on the southern side of the Rhodes Bridge at Rhodes Point. The downside is noise from the railway and roads and the wash of passing ferries etc. This is a refuge from strong winds only.

HOMEBUSH BAY

This is the last substantial bay upriver. Its mouth lies between the Ryde Bridge and Wentworth Point, the latter marked by a tall radio aerial. Factories line both eastern and western shores of the bay, making it so singularly unattractive that it would be profitably bypassed were it not for the Olympic Games developments at its head.

Furthermore it is a shallow bay with a 2-metre-plus channel along its western shore (hug the piles along the seawall for maximum depth) right to the head of the bay where the rusted wrecks there are so old that the mangroves have claimed much of them. The bay gradually shoals from the west to the eastern shore, where it is no more than a metre at low tide if you hug the pylons off that shore — and it's even shallower in parts.

If anchoring, avoid the marine cables about 200 metres in from the mouth of the bay. There is also a canteen about 200 metres down Bennelong Road from the ferry wharf on Wentworth Point, other-wise it's a long hike to shops.

This bay is seriously polluted, so don't even think of fishing: apart from the very real health risks it attracts a hefty fine. In fact, I was reluctant even to sluice the decks with this water, so much has been written about its contamination. The State government was examining a range of proposals to remove or contain the polution at the time of writing, though no clear solution had been posted.

RYDE BRIDGE TO

SILVERWATER BRIDGE

At the risk of offending locals, there is not much to encourage cruising west of the Ryde Bridge. The Parramatta River narrows from this point with dense mangroves to the waters edge broken only by the occasional the house or industrial site. Generally, the ground outside the navigation channel is very, very shallow ground. There is good reason for the channel to be particularly well-lit, with excellent lead marks between navigational marks. Navigate this section with caution: the river is narrow and commercial shipping, particularly the swift rivercats have right of way. Anchoring is not practical, other than in the only (unamed) little bay on the northern shore in this section, where a small jetty and boat ramp are sited. But only shoal draft vessels should consider it.

Whether the approaching Olympics motivated it or not, the new ferry wharves in the area are excellent, the latest being completed at Wentworth Point at the time of writing.

Silverwater Bridge clearance is 12.2 metres. Access is to Rivercats and authorised vessels only.